CENSUS OF INDIA 1931

Census of India 1871-1951, 9 Sets In 384 Bindings (9788121258876) Rs. 700000

Census of India 1931, 28 Vols. In 52 Bindings (9788121271233) Rs. 102000

1. India - Report (9788121276153) Rs. 2820 (Vol. I, Pt. 1)
2. India - Imperial Tables (9788121276139) Rs. 3210 (Vol. I, Pt. 2)
3. India - Ethnographical and Administration Report (9788121276115) Rs. 2900 (Vol. I, Pt. 3 & 5)
4. The Andaman And Nicobar Islands - Report, Tables (9788121276078) Rs. 720 (Vol. II, Pt. 1, Pt. 2)
5. Assam - Report (9788121276054) Rs. 1340 (Vol. III, Pt. 1)
6. Assam - Tables and Administrative Report (9788121276030) Rs. 1830 (Vol. III, Pt. 2 & 3)
7. Baluchistan - Report, Imeprial and Provincial Tables and Administrative Report (9788121276016) Rs. 2320 (Vol. IV, Pt. 1 & 2 & 3)
8. Bengal & Sikkim - Report (9788121275972) Rs. 2860 (Vol. V, Pt. 1)
9. Bengal & Sikkim - Tables (9788121275958) Rs. 1660 (Vol. V, Pt. 2)
10. Calcutta (9788121275910) Rs. 960 (Vol. VI, Pt. 1 & 2)
11. Bengal, Sikkim And Calcutta - Administrative Report (9788121275934) Rs. 580 (Vol. V & VI, Pt. 3)
12. Bihar And Orissa - Report (9788121275897) Rs. 1780 (Vol. VII, Pt. 1)
13. Bihar And Orissa - Tables and Administrative Report (9788121275873) Rs. 1190 (Vol. VII, Pt. 2 & 3)
14. Bombay Presidency - General Report (9788121275835) Rs. 3620 (Vol. VIII, Pt. 1)
15. Bombay - Statistical tables (9788121275811) Rs. 3060 (Vol. VIII, Pt. 2)
16. Bombay Presidency Aden - report and tables and Administrative report (9788121275798) Rs. 520 (Vol. VIII, Pt. 3 & 4)
17. Cities of the Bombay Presidency Report & Statistical tables (9788121275750) Rs. 2020 (Vol. IX, Pt. 1 & 2)
18. The Western India States Agency, In Two Parts - The Report & The Statistical Tables (9788121275736) Rs. 2560 (Vol. X, Pt. 1 & 2)
19. Burma - Report (9788121275712) Rs. 1860 (Vol. XI, Pt. 1)
20. Burma - Tables and Administrative Report (9788121275699) Rs. 1690 (Vol. XI, Pt. 2 & 3)
21. Central Provinces & Berar - Report (9788121275651) Rs. 2340 (Vol. XII, Pt. 1)
22. Central Provinces & Berar - Tables and Administrative Report (9788121275637) Rs. 3120 (Vol. XII, Pt. 2 & 3)
23. Coorg - Report And Tables and Madras - Report (9788121275613) Rs. 2680 (Vol. XIV, Pt. 1)
24. Madras - Imperial And Provincial Tables and The Administration Report (9788121275576) Rs. 1950 (Vol. XIV, Pt. 2 & 4)
25. North - West Frontier Province - Report & Tables (9788121275538) Rs. 2300 (Vol. XV, Pt. 1 & 2)
26. Delhi - Report & Tables (9788121275514) Rs. 1180 (Vol. XVI, Pt. 1 & 2)
27. Punjab - Report (9788121275491) Rs. 2070 (Vol. XVII, Pt. 1)
28. Punjab - Tables (9788121275477) Rs. 1690 (Vol. XVII, Pt. 2)
29. United Provinces of Agra And Oudh - Report (9788121275453) Rs. 3380 (Vol. XVIII, Pt. 1)
30. United Provinces of Agra And Oudh - Imperial And Provincial Tables and Administrative (9788121275439) Rs. 3600 (Vol. XVIII, Pt. 2 & 3)
31. Baroda - Report (9788121275415) Rs. 2800 (Vol. XIX, Pt. 1)
32. Baroda - Tables (9788121275392) Rs. 730 (Vol. XIX, Pt. 2)
33. Baroda - Administrative (9788121275378) Rs. 780 (Vol. XIX, Pt. 3)
34. Central India Agency - Report (9788121275354) Rs. 1690 (Vol. XX, Pt. 1)
35. Central India Agency - Tables and Administrative Volume (9788121275330) Rs. 2260 (Vol. XX, Pt. 2 & 3)
36. Cochin - Report & Tables (9788121275293) Rs. 2460 (Vol. XXI, Pt. 1 & 2 - A & B.)
37. Gwalior - Report (9788121275279) Rs. 1470 (Vol. XXII, Pt. 1)
38. Gwalior - Tables (9788121275255) Rs. 980 (Vol. XXII, Pt. 2)
39. H. E. H. The Nizam's Dominions (Hyderabad State) - Report (9788121275231) Rs. 1540 (Vol. XXIII, Pt. 1)
40. H. E. H. The Nizam's Dominions (Hyderabad State) - Tables (9788121275217) Rs. 1510 (Vol. XXIII, Pt. 2)
41. Jammu & Kashmir State - Report (9788121275194) Rs. 2060 (Vol. XXIV, Pt. 1)
42. Jammu & Kashmir State - Imperial & State Tables (9788121275170) Rs. 1940 (Vol. XXIV, Pt. 2 & 3)
43. Mysore - Report (9788121275156) Rs. 1950 (Vol. XXV, Pt. 1)
44. Mysore - Tables (9788121275132) Rs. 1380 (Vol. XXV, Pt. 2)
45. Ajmer-Merwara - Report And Tables (9788121275118) Rs. 780 (Vol. XXVI)
46. Rajputana Agency And Ajmer-Merwara - Report and Tables and Administrative (9788121275095) Rs. 2380 (Vol. XXVII, Pt. 1 & 2)
47. Travancore - Report (9788121276092) Rs. 2960 (Vol. XXVIII, Pt. 1)
48. Travancore - Tables & Administrative (9788121275996) Rs. 1360 (Vol. XXVIII, Pt. 2 & 4)
49. Jaipur State- Report (9788121275859) Rs. 1280 (Pt. 1)
50. Jaipur State- Tables (9788121275774) Rs. 2030 (Pt. 2)
51. Mayurbhanj state- Report (9788121275675) Rs. 3180 (Pt. 1)
52. Mayurbhanj state- Tables (9788121275552) Rs. 3070 (Pt. 2)

Owing to the antiquity and rarity of this book, certain pages are regrettably absent, and readability is compromised due to the blurring of the original text. If you possess any insights regarding the availability of these missing sections, kindly inform us. Your assistance is crucial in ensuring the completion of this significant work for the benefit of future generations.

CENSUS OF INDIA, 1931

BOOK - 24: VOLUME - XIV

MADRAS

PART II - IMPERIAL AND PROVINCIAL TABLES
PART IV - THE ADMINISTRATION REPORT

M. W. M. YEATTS

GYAN

Published by

Gyan Publishing House
5, Ansari Road
Daryaganj, New Delhi-110002
Phone: 011-47034999, 9811692060
E-mail: books@gyanbooks.com

Distribution Network
gyanbooks.com
India, USA, Canada, UK, Australia

ISBN: 978-81-212-7123-3 (Set) 28 Vols. In 52 Bindings

ISBN: 978-81-212-7557-6 (PB) Vol. XIV, Pt. II & IV

First Published, 1932

2nd Impression 2024

Printed at: Gyan Press, Delhi.

CENSUS OF INDIA 1931

CENSUS OF INDIA, 1931

VOLUME XIV

MADRAS

PART IV

CENSUS OF INDIA, 1931

VOLUME XIV

MADRAS

PART IV

THE ADMINISTRATION REPORT

BY

M. W. M. YEATTS,

OF THE INDIAN CIVIL SERVICE

Superintendent of Census Operations, Madras

MADRAS

PRINTED BY THE SUPERINTENDENT, GOVERNMENT PRESS, AND PUBLISHED BY THE GOVERNMENT OF INDIA CENTRAL PUBLICATION BRANCH, CALCUTTA

1932

CONTENTS

VOLUME XIV—PART IV

THE ADMINISTRATION REPORT

CENSUS OF INDIA, 1931.

MADRAS.

IMPERIAL SERIES, VOLUME XIV, PART IV.

ADMINISTRATION OF THE CENSUS.

CHAPTER I.

ENUMERATION.

Preliminary arrangements. I returned from leave on 9th April 1930 and took charge on the afternoon of the 10th as soon as I arrived in Madras. The records of 1921 were in two large boxes in the Secretariat Central Records and my first care was to sort these out. The collections of circulars and Government Orders and specimen forms were found useful and I have bequeathed similar collections to my 1941 successor. One point noticed, however, was the entire absence of any correspondence from the previous census; all, I was informed, had been destroyed. The great bulk of census correspondence is ephemeral but often points arise which are bound to arise at any census; the record of action taken on them should be preserved for guidance. For example, there was no intimation left that certain officers in the Central Provinces had to be given Telugu schedules and instructions or that Cochin depended upon us for its manuals and slips. There was nothing to show how the manual for supervisors had worked in practice nor suggestions for its improvement in the light of 1921 experience. I have left behind me a full annotated set of circulars and a Supervisors' manual. The 1941 Superintendent will be able from this to see points where difficulties cropped up and will be able to take measures to avoid these during his time of preparation and instruction.

Paper and printing. 2. Census being an entirely central subject this time I was asked to make as much use as possible of central printing and stationery establishments. My experience was not very happy. To begin with, the Stationery Office in Calcutta took three months to comply with my first indent and I had to obtain supplies from the Madras Stationery Office to keep me going.

The buying of paper is closely connected with the location of the press which is to do the printing. When printing is done in Madras it is desirable to buy the paper there too if possible. As regards paper for the schedules however, purchase for all-India by the Census Commissioner is probably preferable. The enormous bulk may produce favourable rates and a superintendent has not enough time after joining duty to arrange the supply of this mass of paper before printing has to begin. In Madras, for example, printing had to be begun in July if the schedules were to be ready for the enumeration. This is only three months after the superintendent takes charge and local firms generally require that much in order to arrange supply. As regards paper for slips however the case is different. If freedom of choice were given the Madras Superintendent could certainly arrange more favourable terms locally. I could have secured the unbleached paper used for slips at an anna a pound cheaper than the price charged me by the Titaghur Mills, in addition to which freight amounting to Rs. 900 was involved by my having to buy in Calcutta. All over, about Rs. 3,500 could probably have been saved had I been able to make a contract for paper from England. Incidentally it is not essential for matters like slips, sorters' tickets and even enumeration schedules that the paper used should be identical throughout India; provided it is adequate for its purpose a certain amount of variation need not arouse objection.

A connected matter is the paper used by local district officers in the preparation of house lists and preliminary enumeration. This is an entirely new debit to the census. Formerly the districts used what paper they had and the census had no concern with supply at this stage: now it has. It is impossible and undesirable to arrange a definite supply to each district for this purpose. Not only do district needs vary but district ideas of economical use vary still more and an incessant sequence of supplemental demands would ensue. What was done was that districts used their own supplies and recouped these from the local stationery office with their next indents; not every district sought recoupment. The extra cost involved by the supply of paper for house lists was Rs. 5,500, including the 10 per cent commission. I have elsewhere suggested that in future censuses enumeration should be a local Government debit and if this suggestion is adopted the paper problem so far as house lists are concerned will disappear. If however this debit remains a central one I would suggest that the policy followed this time is the most convenient, most saving of correspondence and freight, and most economical in use. The variation in district demands was most noticeable. A similar variation in economy and efficiency could be observed in practically every census sphere.

The special unemployment schedules, sorters' tickets and compilation registers were printed at the Government of India Press but not the ordinary enumeration schedules or the Report or Tables. I do not see how it can ever be possible for any Government of India Press to print satisfactorily millions of schedules in Tamil, Telugu, Malayalam and Kanarese, though possibly in future Oriya schedules might be procured from the Calcutta press. The printing of circle lists was done either at the Government Press or any local press, whichever was cheaper. Such at least were my original orders. The Central Printing Office, however, required such printing to be done always at a Government Press if possible. I do not see any real justification for this. There are in most Madras districts and certainly in all the larger ones, competent private presses eminently suited for the production of job work; the west coast is particularly well off in this regard; traditions of fine printing have long been established there and the standard of typography is high though charges are very moderate. Another request by the Central Printing Office was that a specimen of every piece of printing done by private presses should accompany their bills sent for sanction, e.g., a copy of every circle list was to be sent — there are 20,000 odd circles in this presidency. It was not till I pointed out that this would involve very heavy postage charges both ways, while one circle list was surely an adequate sample of the class of printing provided, that these rigid orders were modified. A single instance will show how ridiculous and costly insistence on the use of Government of India presses by Madras may be. The carriage on one batch of sorters' tickets from Delhi to Mangalore was alone greater than the figure for which I could have had them printed (including cost of paper) by a Mangalore printing firm.

The Census Commissioner first required that all English forms should be printed at the Government of India Press, although the vernacular ones were being printed in Madras. Whether such a dispersion of effort is desirable at all is open to doubt but another consideration required the abandonment of this proposal. The Government of India Press declined to send out the forms direct to the various recipients over the 26 districts of the presidency. This meant therefore that my office would have had to do the unpacking, repacking and despatch of all these forms over the presidency and bear the extra freight involved. Realization of this brought about printing at Madras of English forms along with the vernacular ones.

It is probable that by 1941 provinces will be much more independent of the Government of India than they are now; if however, the census is then also run as a purely central matter I strongly urge that the Superintendent be given wider discretion in sanctioning such matters as local printing and purchase of stationery. Much correspondence was involved by the procedure requiring Delhi or Calcutta sanction to straightforward matters of local supply. All stationery should be obtained from the local stationery office and all printing done at the Madras Government Press or in the case of circle lists at the most convenient local press whose charges prove lower than those of the Government Press. The ten per cent commission charged by provincial stationery offices should be waived in this case.

I suggest as one of the first steps to be taken by the Census Commissioner on his appointment, the arrangement of special terms with the railway companies for freight of census parcels. Railway freight came to Rs. 4,500 this time and that despite the free use I made of sea carriage.

Enumeration.

3. The general scheme followed that of previous years. A separate census chain was formed working through block, circle and charge to join the ordinary administrative sequence with the taluk. Enumerators were chosen for blocks, supervisors for circles and charge superintendents for charges. The census was once again based on a house list. Undoubtedly so long as the block system is followed and outside enumerators appointed the preparation of house lists is essential. By no other means could a reasonable guarantee be achieved against overlapping or omission by spare-time enumerators. The making of these house lists is however a matter of considerable complexity and expense. This is particularly the case in the larger towns and a very considerable problem indeed in Madras city. Definite consideration should be applied next time to see how far municipal numbers can be used in census enumeration. This is a matter for preliminary enquiry, not one which a superintendent can carry out within his brief term. He has no time for experiment but must get immediately on with actual performance. I asked municipalities to consider how far their numbering system might be used in census enumeration having regard to the importance of accuracy and definiteness. The replies showed that there was less possibility of help in this direction than I had anticipated. Numbering systems in municipalities are not exhaustive because houses which are exempt from taxation whether because of no valuation, municipal ownership, being educational or religious institutions, etc., are not given a number. From a census point of view any place where a human being may be found on the census night should be visited and therefore should appear in the house list and be numbered. It might be possible to use the municipal numbering in certain areas and prepare a house list for others but there is distinct risk of confusion and so long as the usual type of house list is in question, it would be better to adhere to a completely separate list. In municipalities, however, these lists should be drawn up and the division into blocks and circles made by the municipal officers who know the regions in question. The same officers should be entrusted with the recommendation of suitable enumerators; they are more likely to know the peculiar conditions of each region and the men best acquainted with them than tahsildars who have no direct administrative connection.

One innovation was to alter the definition of a house. For demographic purposes what we should bear in mind is the independent dwelling. This has no essential connection with a building at all. I found a good deal of misconception as to meaning of the new definition and on the other hand very quick comprehension of what it involved, both in the most unlikely quarters. Often a village officer had grasped the essentials at once in making his list while the presumably more intelligent supervisor had misunderstood. I recommend, however, a continuance of this definition. 1941 will find it no longer a novelty and the idea will probably be better appreciated. It is unwise to take anything for granted in expounding these points. It did not occur to me that there could be any misconception over the word 'dwelling'. I was mistaken. Any definition given in a census circular or manual should be gone through very closely and even the most apparently obvious terms explained and illustrated.

The use of household schedules in Madras city and in Bangalore was given up. I carried out a good deal of preparatory work to this end particularly among the European community who had invariably been given household schedules in the past. The departure was well received and was a great success. So far as Europeans were concerned the enumerators in Madras city and Bangalore had nothing but good to say of their reception. The only comment one or two made was that it was sometimes difficult to get past the butler or other domestic and I recommend to my 1941 successor that in his exhortations to the public he should ask all persons maintaining domestic servants to issue strict injunctions that the arrival of the census enumerator is to be intimated immediately to the master or mistress of the house. It might be a good idea to have a card printed for enumerators in such areas rather on the lines of the ordinary commercial traveller's. It could have advertisements on the back.

I recommend the total abolition of household schedules. I cannot see that any need for their retention exists in Madras presidency where a knowledge of English is so widespread. If here and there in a mufassal town or village there lives some European or other person insufficiently acquainted with the vernacular to understand questioning by an enumerator who lacks English, all that is necessary is for the supervisor of the circle himself to enumerate such persons. This could be easily done as one of the incidents of ordinary control. The use of household schedules has led to a good many omissions in the past, as well as to a large number of unintelligible and useless entries. It may be said that household schedules should be retained for the use of upper-class passengers in trains but I cannot see that even this is necessary, as on the census night in Madras many first-class passengers, Europeans and Indians, were enumerated in the ordinary way like their humbler fellow-travellers without any difficulty whatever. For this class of enumeration I recommend ordinary schedules in English.

Census superintendents may expect as regards indents for schedule forms an almost universal tendency to excessive demand. I give as Appendix I a copy of a letter issued to all Collectors which speaks for itself. Here again, the district variation already referred to more than once was notable. The original supply calculated on a 10 per cent increase in the population (a very close forecast) was almost certainly adequate, save perhaps in a few exceptional spots. Any local variation could easily be made up by census officers introducing flexibility into their arrangements and control. Enumeration books are deliberately so bound that sheets can be easily either added or detached. Obviously, therefore, every supervisor has a means at his hand of adjusting the supply of schedule forms among his enumerators: similar flexibility should exist between circles under the direction of the charge superintendent and so on. An intelligent man who has done preliminary enumeration on plain paper is surely not going to be baffled at the final enumeration if he finds his printed forms inadequate. The sub-registrar of Vatlagundu in Madura, a charge superintendent, showed excellently what could be done by the exercise of thought. The main argument for issuing census books ready made is that the Government Press can bind them up in large numbers at speed. I should be inclined to try next time the issue of schedules in single sheets, separate from the covers. The supervisors would then issue schedules calculated on the numbers of the preliminary enumeration. Thus automatically they would have the balance in their hands instead of most of it being locked up in books from which lack of initiative or distance prevents it being rescued.

There was a good deal of difficulty in some places in getting men for the various census posts. This difficulty is likely to increase as the decades go on. Several applications for general exemption were made, e.g., by Health Officers and doctors and post office establishments. Preposterous over-statement frequently characterized the applications. Thus one District Medical Officer drew a harrowing picture of the district bestrewn with corpses as a result of two sub-assistant surgeons being appointed supervisors in areas where they were the only qualified persons. Ordinarily, of course, doctors and such persons will not be appointed but in the peculiar conditions obtaining in parts of India it may be that some sub-assistant surgeon is the only possible choice unless some one is to be brought from 40 to 50 miles. In such cases it is absurd not to use him. The Madras Government supported me and declined to give general exemptions. This principle is most important; census requires the co-operation of other departments and the total exemption of one category of public servants is not likely to induce readiness on the part of others not so favoured. There is no man so busy as not to have some spare time and census work is spare-time work. Apart possibly from the army and police it should be laid down by the Government of India that no general exemptions are to be given. Every case should be decided individually. The one case in which a general exemption was given this time (not by me) was that of officers of a Central Department, the Post Office. In what way a post office clerk differs from any other Government clerk in the sense that he cannot be given spare-time employment is far from clear and had I known of the application made by postal clerks of Salem to be relieved of census work I should have opposed it. Neither the Municipal Chairman nor the Collector nor the Postmaster-General however informed me what was going on and in the end, greatly to the inconvenience of the Chairman of Salem Municipality, post office clerks were under the orders of the Collector relieved of their duties. Subsequently these clerks were induced only with difficulty to return the books they had originally been given ar d so facilitate the completion of the work they had evaded. Census work in India has on the whole been in the past unpaid and can, I think, be kept so provided that all departments of Government are made to realize that they must lend a hand. The consciousness that everyone is involved frequently brings a greater acceptance of difficulties or tasks. It is particularly important that officers of Central Departments should lead the way in census service.

A special appointment was made at this census for Ganjam. This reflected the Oriya-Telugu agitation there and the probable advent of an Enquiry Committee on the lines sketched by the Simon Report. Experience showed the wisdom of an appointment of this sort where conflicting influences tend to meet on the census enumeration. Suggestions were made that quasi-political questions should be asked in the census. I opposed this resolutely: every interest requires that a census enumeration should be as objective as possible. If some political preference or problem is in question let a plebiscite *ad hoc* be taken. To tack it on to a census enumeration would be merely to affect the credence attached to the census facts without obtaining an absolute solution of the problem in question.

I suggested to the Madras Government that free use might be made of Assistant Collectors at the census. I pointed out that supervision and practice of enumeration would teach these youths much about their district and its language and customs, knowledge for which their probationary course is actually intended. I would go further and suggest that the census report (including the Administrative Volume) and statistics of the province be added to the list of books which all Assistant Collectors, Police probationers, etc., are expected to study for their promotion examinations. Copies will be available in every district headquarters.

Instructions to enumerators.

4. Madras has never gone in for issuing a census code in the shape of a single book; it has preferred to issue separate circulars on various phases. I followed this course but have laid down a definite order in which circulars should be retained in every district, the three Indian States, Bangalore and in Coorg, and have issued to each a stout jacket in which to bind these circulars. The paging is the same everywhere; any page number will have the same meaning in any district of the presidency and can be quoted readily. A small octavo-sized code is to be preferred if it could be issued at the very beginning once for all, but the fragmentary way in which instructions are received, e.g., those relating to census on railways, of troops, etc., make it impossible to issue a single book at the outset. For separate circulars semi-foolscap is probably the best size but next time I should be inclined to experiment with octavo which is more conveniently carried.

Instructions to enumerators were kept down to a minimum. It is fatal to look upon the enumerator as an office and to load him with printed matter. The ideal should be for the written instructions given to an enumerator to be reduced to the absolute minimum and to concentrate his training upon actual practice. This means that supervisors should be carefully trained and they in turn should set their enumerators on the true path. Taking enumerators for what they are, masses of printing mislead them more often than not. This is particularly the case in Madras where no fewer than five languages besides English have to be used in schedules.

I would abolish the sample entries altogether in the schedule books; instead of these being taken merely as guides they were in many cases taken as laws and this attitude will persist. Sample entries in English can be given in the Supervisors' Manual but for the enumerator they are inadvisable.

I had some difficulty over translations of the illustrative examples in the schedule and found that the Malayalam ones in particular were far from happy although they had been prepared and passed by a local committee in Malabar. This is another argument for cutting down the illustrative element in the schedules to the absolute minimum. We can then make sure that our intentions are not being belied by unhappy translations.

The schedule itself ought, I think, to be in the hands of the superintendent some months before it is necessary for the press to begin printing. He could thus think over it, discuss it, practise it, and evolve useful criticisms. A meeting of provincial superintendents should be held before printing is begun so that suggested changes can be discussed and the final form of the schedule settled and procedure arranged. More attention should be paid to the way the headings are printed. The important words should be in heavier type. Choice of phrase should be very carefully made; for example, the term 'occupation' should be given up entirely and the phrase 'Means of livelihood' substituted. This gives a far truer rendering of the type of information we really want under this head and is susceptible of an immediate and accurate translation into all South Indian languages. It is most important to bear in mind the class of person who is going to perform the actual enumeration. Thus a word like 'industry' offers great difficulties and only much thought and actual practice will enable it to be properly expounded to the average enumerator and apprehended by him. This word is not really translatable to men of his type except by paraphrase and explanation: the single word translators produce is Greek to him.

Supervisors' Manual.

5. I drew up a manual for supervisors similar to that for 1921. I recommend the preparation of such a manual again in 1941 but the enumeration book enclosed with it should invariably be in English; the practice of binding a vernacular copy of the schedule with the manual while theoretically excellent, has grave defects in practice. I came across several cases where Tamil officers serving in Telugu tracts and vice versa and similarly men of other vernaculars could speak well the language of the area in which they served but could not read or write it readily; yet they were obvious and desirable choices for supervisors. All of them knew English well. Such cases were particularly common in railway areas. In Madras Presidency it should always be possible to find an English-knowing supervisor and I strongly recommend that the manual and any enclosures to it should be in English from beginning to end. I have left behind as already mentioned a fully annotated copy of the 1931 manual. The main general points I would urge here besides that already given is that a scheme of instruction should be laid down with details and illustrations to guide supervisors in their training of enumerators. Wide personal experience has shown me that even a stupid enumerator is capable of grasping his duties when they are put to him with the real underlying purpose made clear. Too many supervisors throw off their instructions in a routine manner and such instruction is accepted by the enumerator in the same fashion. The great desiderata in a census are an absolutely objective approach, abolishing all preconceptions, grasping the real object behind our activities, making sure that the queries are understood by the person enumerated and recording them in clear and unequivocal language in the schedules. The Golden Rule in census enumeration is: every entry in any census document should be such that it will convey a single identical meaning wherever and whenever read, to whomsoever reads it. To save writing, I recommend that a full list of contractions in the various languages for such items as district names (e.g., Vizag., Coimb., Trichy., N.A.), languages (Ori., Tel., Tam.), answers regarding literacy and certain other points be drawn out. I found some enumerators writing down the long Tamil phrase which is the only equivalent of the single word 'Literate'. A single system could be expounded and used by everybody. I introduced such contractions during my tours

but it would be better in future for the Superintendent to draw them up before ever instruction began. There need be no fear of such contractions being abused. No contraction should be allowed which might produce obscurity; e.g., Mad. might be Madras or Madura; but that is merely a matter of care in drawing up the list. I found enumerators take very kindly indeed to, e.g. திருச்சி, విశా, బి. ఒ., for Trichinopoly, Vizagapatam, Bihar and Orissa respectively. It is essential that the list be standardized and taught as part of the general instructions. I was asked several times what a census supervisor or charge superintendent should do about his own enumeration on census night. The answer was that these officers were not bona fide travellers and that they should ensure that they were reckoned as present in their normal habitations on that night and not enumerated elsewhere. This should be categorically stated in the 1941 manual or what corresponds to it.

Non-synchronous tracts.

6. As in 1921 synchronous enumeration was not possible in certain tracts. These are set out in G.O. No. 4285, Law (General), dated 8th October 1930. Instructions as in 1921 were issued to govern the treatment of areas affected by plague or where evacuation was a possibility from other causes. No cases of large festivals on census night were reported. There were, however, some small festivals attracting persons from a few miles around. In these I ordered that there was no need to have a special festival enumeration. All that was required was for a person said on census night to be at such a festival to be counted as resident in his ordinary home, and only those persons who came from a distance outside the festival range were enumerated as travellers in the village. Special festival enumerations give much extra work and are to be avoided wherever possible. This is possible in the case of local festivals. In one case I was told by apprehensive municipal officers that the real difficulty was not so much with the large number of persons as the intoxication in which the majority would be found on the night and the consequent fear of trouble. A small extension of the non-synchronous area had to be made owing to the omission of a village in Ramnad from the ordinary enumeration. This was discovered by my office during the preparation of village statistics and an enumeration as for 26th February 1931, was immediately ordered and the results incorporated. I recommend particular attention to the Ramnad-Sivaganga estate parts of this district. Control seems to be weak, village names repeat and change and all over, this area gave more trouble and worry than the rest of the presidency put together. Tirupattur taluk was worst of all.

Railway census.

7. Particular attention was devoted to the railway census and we succeeded in enlisting the interest of the railway companies. I went over the larger stations in the presidency in consultation with the local Transportation Superintendents and decided which trains should be taken for enumeration purposes. Arrangements were made for the Central, Egmore and Basin Bridge stations in Madras, for Trichinopoly, for Podanur, for Bezwada, Guntakal and a number of others. Certain trains need not be checked at all. Examples are the short distance trains leaving Madras about 6 p.m. and carrying mainly season-ticket holders going home after the day's work. These trains would have been extremely difficult to check because of the large numbers travelling and the great rush; nor did I think it worth the trouble of taking them, having regard to the fact that all the passengers were merely returning home and would be in their houses that evening. I gave a general instruction that no person travelling back on a season ticket need be included as a traveller on census night. These points should all be set forth categorically in the 1941 instructions and I recommend that the same close touch be kept with railway administrations. In several cases railway officers like Balaam came to curse and remained to bless; many took a real interest in census enumeration work and assisted considerably in making their subordinates interested and efficient. The great thing to remember with the railway staff is that they observe a peculiar attitude of detachment from the ordinary revenue administration and unless their own superiors show that they are interested in census work and expect railway subordinates to take their share, no census superintendent can look for anything but a lukewarm interest in what must seem to the railway subordinate an outside activity.

Acknowledgments. 8. How best to acknowledge the services of those who worked in the census occasioned some difficulty. My original intention was to send the same holograph letter to every person who performed unpaid census duties, no distinction being made on the basis of alleged differences in performance. These last are always difficult to assess in a matter like this and it is better to eschew any attempts to do so. Retrenchment considerations entered here however as elsewhere and forced reconsideration. Clearly the numbers had to be cut down. Census officers were therefore divided into (i) servants of Government or Local Boards and (ii) non-officials. Collectors were asked to submit lists of those who had done particularly good work. For persons in category (i) mentioned in these lists, I secured recognition in the form of a good service entry in their conduct sheets. This step had the approval of the Government of Madras. In the case of non-officials I issued a standard holograph sanad. No differentiation in form of sanad was observed.

Here and there some non-officials did work quite out of the ordinary, e.g., when they printed schedule headings at their own expense in order to help their enumerators with preliminary enumeration. To such men I wrote personally in addition to giving a sanad. These cases however were very rare.

The proper recognition of census service will always be difficult. Government servants will ordinarily prefer a good service entry to a sanad, as helping them more in their careers. Sanads should be uniform in content and get-up. Any attempt at discrimination is undesirable and conversations with a good many soldiers of my census army convinced me that a standard form of recognition was more appreciated.

Public attitude. 9. Considerable apprehensions were entertained in many quarters as to the attitude of the general public having regard to the Civil Disobedience and other campaigns rife at the time. There were two sources of possible trouble, (1) misconception that the census enquiry had some fiscal object in view and (2) pure desire to obstruct the Government. No. (1) was never very strong in Madras though cases did occur ; nor did No. (2) amount in the end to very much. The census had everything to gain by publicity and from the beginning I invoked the assistance of the press and kept them informed of the progress of the operations. Notices were put up in the village chattrams in the vernacular and also in third-class carriages and on railway platforms giving the main facts about the census, stressing the point of its secrecy and the duty of all concerned, while not forgetting to mention the obligation imposed on the citizen to answer truly the questions. Copies of the notices put up in railway stations and in the compartments are in the files. One or two men in Nellore offered to give trouble but all came round in the end and did their duty as enumerators. One man in Malabar had to be prosecuted for encouraging resistance to census activities but this case was largely mixed up with general political subversiveness and was not a purely census phenomenon. Some difficulty came from Gujeratis in Madras city but by dint of persuasion and argument these were overcome and the information extracted without the need for resorting to prosecution. I think that the South Indian and certainly the Tamilian is much too hard-headed to be misled by anti-census activities. He has no lack of shrewd common sense and if we appeal to this common sense we shall never have cause to regret it.

Difficulties arose over the production of census schedules in court. The Census Act of 1929 protected these schedules only against production (*a*) in any civil court and (*b*) in certain quasi-civil procedure in the criminal courts. Several requests were made for information and summonses received from criminal and other courts. Census information is collected on a strictly confidential basis. This was emphasized during my tours and all other officers instructed to emphasize it equally. I was consistently averse to allowing these schedules to be produced. Ultimately the Government of India decided against this view. Only once however was production found inevitable. In other cases the schedules had all been destroyed before the question of production was settled. In the case where they were produced I arranged with the High Court that the procedure in their regard should be for the schedules not to be filed with the ordinary documents but kept in a sealed cover, to be consulted by the Judge if necessary. If in his opinion the entry of any census detail on the record was required only that part relevant to the case should be so entered. Ordinarily only private individuals wished production of census schedules. One case from East Godavari concerned a prosecution under the Child Marriage Restraint Act but here also the origin of the prosecution lay in personal animus.

Future Census Acts should, I think, protect census schedules against compulsory production in any court or public proceeding whatever.

Since census detail is confidential it is as important to control the fate of the rough schedules as of the fair. Instructions were issued at this census for the care, collection, storage and destruction of the rough enumeration schedules which in previous years had been the subject of no specific regulation. Supervisors were instructed to collect all rough schedules after the final enumeration and deposit them in the taluk offices. Deputy Superintendents were instructed to direct each taluk officer to destroy the rough schedules when copying and check of the taluk or other unit in question were completed. The benefits of this care of the rough schedules were illustrated in Malabar, for some of the fair schedules for Walluvanad taluk were eaten by white ants in transit; the rough schedules were called for and abstraction completed from them.

Deputy Superintendents should be instructed on similar lines in future censuses and told to issue destruction orders as soon as a taluk or municipality has been fully copied and checked. They should call for an acknowledgment from all the persons concerned that such destruction has been completely effected.

Suggestions for next census.

10. I have already in a letter to the Census Commissioner (No. 2154-1, dated 11th April 1931) suggested the desirability of a change in the census date. I shall not recapitulate the arguments put forth in that letter but shall sketch the scheme which should govern the taking of a Madras census.

If the census were held in the first half of September it would mean that the three or four months immediately preceding it coincided with a comparatively quiet time for the village and revenue staff. The Madras system lends itself peculiarly to census operations, provided a suitable time is chosen; whence my proposal. The village itself should be the unit and the village officer or the accountant the enumerator. Thus there is no need to appoint outside enumerators or to train them and probably no need for the house or block list unless a house list is desired for its own sake. The preliminary enumeration could be started in June or earlier and supervised by the Revenue Inspector, Tahsildar, or other officers in their normal rounds. The final enumeration (presuming that the *de facto* system is retained) could be done during the course of the actual census day, not only the night, for in the ordinary village areas any changes to be recorded will be known then. Another possibility is that for final enumeration alone volunteers might be enlisted. I do not think that there would be any difficulty in getting men for one night's work, which actually would resolve itself into comparatively few entries. As the karnam's preliminary entries were approved he could write out the sorting slips there and then. Immediately after the census and after the despatch of the provisional totals, the karnam would write up slips for the hitherto unrecorded entries and cancel those for entries deleted. A small honorarium should be given to each village officer for enumeration work.

Abstraction would so far as rural areas are concerned have been practically finished by the census date and sorting could begin straight off. It should be done at district headquarters by a detachment of 50 karnams for each district, that is to say, about 4 or 5 for a taluk. These men would be under the control of a specially selected Revenue Inspector. The Revenue Inspectors would have to be nominated well in advance and previously trained by the Superintendent in person. They should proceed to train their karnams and go on with the sorting. Compilation would be done in a central office in Madras. The karnams could be paid a small fee for census work, say Rs. 10

to Rs. 15 a month for sorting subject to a prescribed outturn. The Revenue Inspector should draw a considerable special pay, say 50 per cent of his normal emoluments. The man chosen for this post should be one of the most promising men in the district.

It seems to me that this system would bring the census into much closer accord with the organic features of the administration. The men copying and sorting the slips would be district men whose ordinary work as village officer gives them a close acquaintance with district terminology and difficulties. The officer at the head of the sorting office would also be a district man. Theoretically, the ideal would be to have sorting done at each taluk head-quarters ; the difficulty of this, however, is in the supervision. There are 250 taluks in the Madras Presidency and it would not be possible to make sure of adequate supervision over all. The Superintendent could easily train 26 to 30 men ; he could not do likewise for 250.

I had hoped to adopt a system of the above kind this year but was forced to abandon the notion. The times were too difficult, and district officers too overworked and harassed by political problems for fundamental experiments to be possible. In any case, with a February census date, village officers could not possibly be given all their villages to enumerate during the two months preceding the census date nor could they be spared for copying or sorting in the two or three months succeeding it.

In every village where there is a school, the local schoolmaster could if necessary be ordered to take part of the village as enumerator.

There are great advantages in using as few enumerators as possible. To obtain an objective scientific record we want to eliminate personal error as far as possible. At present, we have 400,000 enumerators. By training them on uniform lines we try to reduce their personal variation as much as possible but there must remain a considerable scope for idiosyncrasy. By using the village staff we could for the rural areas carry out our enumeration with only 60,000. That is to say that instead of 400,000 personal errors we only have 60,000. A further advantage is that these headmen and karnams are village officers under the control of Government and are therefore likely to be more amenable to discipline and control. Each would copy his own village details and would sort them and also those of villages in his neighbourhood ; thus his local knowledge would be used to the full.

It would not always be possible to do this in the larger towns. To some extent, however, larger blocks could be given and the time for preliminary enumeration extended. In the same way slips could be copied from the approved preliminary enumeration. Even if however the present procedure had to be followed more or less unaltered for the larger towns, the changes above proposed cover by far the greater part of the country and those areas in which enumerators are most difficult to find. It is not possible to give a close estimate of the cost of such proposals but a rough estimate at the present rates would be half this year's figure.

The degree of unpaid effort associated with an Indian census is one of its most remarkable features and is greatly to the credit of the country. Probabilities are that disinclination to take up such duties will increase. This was observed by my predecessor in 1921 and by myself. As a result of the heavy cuts made in my budget, travelling allowance had to be cut down to the bare minimum, the process beginning with myself. I made every endeavour to deal uniformly with the 26,000 odd bills received, applying an actual expenses basis. Complaints were however numerous and it is possible that a re-collection of severe audit applied in 1931 may tend to increase disinclination for census duties. This fact constitutes a further argument in favour of breaking away from the hitherto accepted practice and adopting some such scheme as that outlined above.

The Madras census army on the move on 26th February 1931 night was about half a million strong. This gives some idea of the complexity of the arrangements involved by the census on a *de facto* basis. The system can be continued only so long as the enumerating staff works voluntarily. This is bound to decrease as time goes on and whether it is worth while continuing the *de facto* system is open to doubt. The United States does not attempt to do so and achieves probably quite as accurate a determination on a *de jure* basis. The Madras ryotwari system is peculiarly suited to the United States manner and if to this change could be added a time more suitable to the revenue administration, the Madras census would be an easier undertaking for all concerned. The *de facto* method involves great complexities on railways and communication. These would be much simplified in the alternative method.

11. It is my impression that the urban element in Madras has been under-estimated. For new inclusions the Superintendent has inevitably to depend mainly upon recommendations of Collectors. These officers vary much in the attention they give to the usual request for suggestions. It would probably help if concrete proposals were put to them for consideration, and a tentative list based on 1931 experience has been included among the records retained. I would suggest that the names in it be sent to the respective Collectors as soon as my successor takes charge in 1940 and opinion invited whether they should be treated as towns. (See sample letter printed for guidance as Appendix II.) The Registrar-General of Panchayats, or whatever officer corresponds to him in 1940, might also be consulted. The Superintendent should visit as many of these places as possible. In the last resort it is his opinion which is decisive and he should try to inspect all doubtful cases. The selection given is solely of towns above 5,000 or near it which appear to possess urban characteristics. There are others over 5,000 not included because of no apparent possession now of such characteristics. These may have developed however by 1940 and I suggest that village statistics be scrutinized then and additions be considered in the light of 1940 conditions.

In general, when dealing with Collectors and district officers it is best to give wherever possible a specific suggestion for opinion. This will generally be dealt with on its merits and a useful reply received. General invitations for suggestions receive a very varying treatment and only officers who are interested devote much thought and trouble to their answer.

APPENDIX I.

OFFICE OF THE SUPERINTENDENT
OF CENSUS OPERATIONS,

MADRAS,

Triplicane, 19th January 1931.

C. Let. No. 1057-1.

From

M. W. W. M. YEATTS, ESQ., I.C.S.,
SUPERINTENDENT OF CENSUS OPERATIONS,
Madras,

To

ALL COLLECTORS.

SIR,

[Census—Enumeration schedules—Supply.]

In paragraphs 5 and 6 of Circular No. 21, I appealed for a closer scrutiny of supplemental indents. The appeal has had little effect. I am receiving applications every day of the most extravagant nature which show either a completely inadequate original indent or a completely unconsidered supplemental request. Thus asks for 100 additional books. That is enough for the enumeration of 24,000 people and the total population of the town is only 40,000 odd. The Tahsildar of with about 3,000 people in view asks for one book of 12 sheets for every 25 units of the floating population and makes the modest total request of 250 additional books. 60,000 people could be enumerated in 250 books. In addition he asks for 750 loose schedules (on which 15,000 people could be enumerated). The Tahsildar of demands 100 more books in peremptory tones, saying that preliminary enumeration is at a standstill because of lack of books. If it is, it is no credit to him, because preliminary enumeration is not dependent on books at all. I have just been inspecting thoroughly satisfactory preliminary enumeration in the Ceded Districts where no printed paper was used at all.

All these requests make free use of such words as 'forthwith', 'immediate', 'totally inadequate', etc. If anything is totally inadequate it is the consideration these officers have given to the whole affair from original indent onwards. I cannot possibly direct the press to comply with such reckless indents and once more I would earnestly request Collectors and all other persons concerned to give real study to the problem before hurling in furious last-minute indents. One single sheet should suffice for 20 persons, one book for 240. Do not go by the number of houses alone, for one effect of the new definition of a 'house' is inevitably to increase greatly the number of houses without however affecting the population. Schedule requirements should therefore be estimated on the latter which can be known quite closely enough from the last census statistics.

I have the honour to be,

Sir,

Your most obedient servant,

T. B. SUBRAHMANYAM,

for *Superintendent of Census operations.*

APPENDIX II.

Sample letter regarding treatment of places as towns.

I should be glad of your suggestions on the following point.

2. Ordinarily the population minimum for places treated as towns for the census statistics is 5,000. To qualify for treatment as a town, however, the possession of definite urban characteristics is required. The places mentioned in the enclosed list were not recommended by local officers to be treated as towns at the 1931 census. They now possess however populations exceeding 5,000 or very little below. I should be obliged if you would give me your opinion whether any of these places possess definite urban characteristics and are likely in your opinion to merit treatment as towns in 1941. The unit in question is the true urban aggregation. This may, and frequently does, consist of portions of different revenue villages. Where a definite urban aggregation exists, steps are taken at census time to secure separate enumeration of the urban part regardless of the number of revenue villages which may contribute to it. Thus, the possible Chatrapur town contemplated in the list enclosed would consist of Sitaramapalli village and parts of some adjacent ones. Places which are definitely mere overgrown villages should not be considered for town treatment merely on account of a population exceeding 5,000.

Number and district. (1)	Taluk. (2)	Place. (3)
1. Ganjam Plains.	Chatrapur ..	Chatrapur.
		Purushottapur.
	Berhampur ..	Digopohandi.
	Chicacolo ..	Calingapatam.
		Amadalavalsa.
		Varanasi.
	Tekkali. ..	Kasibugga *cum* Palasa.
		Mandasa.
2. Vizagapatam Plains.	Anakapalle ..	Kasimkota.
	Vizianagram ..	Nellimarla.
3. Godavari, East.	Amalapuram ..	Komaragiripatnam.
		Mummidivaram.
		Perur.
	Rajahmundry.	Kottapalle.
	Razole ..	Manipallo.
		Razole.
		Kottapeta.
4. West Godavari.	Bhimavaram ..	Gunupudi.
		Undi.
		Viravasaramu.
		Akuvidu.
	Ellore	Pulla.
	Narsapur ..	Yellamanchili.
	Tanuku ..	Velpuru.
5. Kistna ..	Divi	Gantasala.
6. Guntur ..	Tenali	Kattivaram.
	Bapatla ..	Chinna Ganjam.
	Guntur ..	Ankireddipalem.
		Tadikonda.
	Ongole.. ..	Tanguturu.
	Repalle ..	Nizampatam.*
7. Nellore ..	Atmakur ..	Atmakur.
	Udayagiri ..	Udayagiri.
8. Cuddapah.	Cuddapah ..	Chennur.
	Rajampet ..	Koduru.
9. Kurnool ..	Pattikonda ..	Pattikonda.
		Maddikara.
	Dhone ..	Dhone.
	Kurnool ..	Kodamuru.
		Gudur.
	Markapur ..	Markapur.
	Cumbum ..	Cumbum.
	Koilkuntla ..	Koilkuntla.
	Nandikotkur ..	Atmakur.
		Nandikotkur.
10. Bellary ..	Siruguppa ..	Tekkalakota.
11. Anantapur.	Gooty	Kona Kondla.
12. North Arcot.	Gudiyattam ..	Darapadavedu.
		Katpadi.
	Walajapet ..	Timiri.
13. Salem ..	Krishnagiri ..	Kavoripatnam.
	Namakkal ..	Paramati.
	Tiruchongodu.	Arasiramani.
		Idanganasalai.
		Kumarapalaiyam.
14. Coimbatore.	Avanashi ..	Avanashi.
	Bhavani ..	Andiyur.
		Brahmadesam.
		Jambai.
		Kavundappadi.
		Kurichchi.
		Olagadam.
		Tiruppur.
	Coimbatore ..	Kuniyamuttur.
		Savuripalaiyam.
		Singanallur.
		Tirumalaiyampalaiyam.
		Vellalur.
	Dharapuram ..	Kangayam.
		Kulattupalaiyam.
		Mulanur.
		Nandavanampalaiyam.
		Vellakovil.
	Erode	Perundurai.
	Gobichettipalaiyam.	Nambiyur.
		Siruvalur.
	Palladam ..	Sulur.
	Pollachi ..	Vettaigarampudur.
15. South Arcot.	Tirukkoyilur ..	Sendamangalam.
	Villupuram ..	Kottaikuppam.
16. Tanjore ..	Kumbakonam.	Maruttuvakudi.
17. Trichinopoly.	Musiri	Musiri.
	Perambalur.	Arumbavur.
	Udaiyarpalaiyam.	Vilandai.

* Nizampatam was recommended by the district officers for exclusion in 1931. Its population has however attained over 6,000 and despite its declining importance it may possibly still be considered. It has old historic importance.

The inclusion of Kiranur and Alangudi in Pudukkottai was at the special request of the State authorities. Their inclusion next time should depend upon a careful scrutiny of their size and urban characteristics.

The retention of Rajampet in Cuddapah should be considered. Probably, however, the low 1931 population is not representative.

Number and district. (1)	Taluk. (2)	Place. (3)
18. Madura ..	Dindigul ..	Attur.
		Tadikombu.
		Vedasandur.
	Periyakulam ..	Melmangalam.
		Pannaippuram.
		Tamaraikkulam.
		Tirumarasanayakanur.
		Ammapatti.
19. Ramnad ..	Srivilliputtur ..	Sundarapandiyam.
		Nattampatti.
20. Tinnevelly.	Nanguneri ..	Tisaiyanvilai.
	Sankaranayinarkovil.	Rayagiri.
		Serndamangalam.
		Viswanathapperi.
	Srivaikuntam.	Sawyerpuram.
	Tenkasi ..	Kilappavur.
		Vadagarai—Kil Pidagai.
		Chokkampatti.
	Tiruchendur ..	Paramankurichchi.
21. Nilgiris ..	Coonoor ..	Ketti.
22. Malabar ..	Calicut ..	Chevayur.
	Chirakkal ..	Alikkod.
		Payyanur.
		Kunnimangalam.
	Ernad	Feroke.
		Kondotti.
		Manjeri.
		Nilambur.
		Tirurangadi.
		Parappangadi.
	Palghat ..	Kunisseri.
		Kotuvayur.
		Putusseri.
	Ponnani ..	Chavakkad.
		Tirur.
	Kottayam ..	Kuttuparamba.
	Kurumbranad.	Pantalayini—Quilandi.
23. South Kanara.	Kasaragod ..	Cheruvattur.
		Nileshwar.
		Pallikara.
		Trikaripur.
	Udipi	Malpe.

I.—Census Divisions and Agency.

S. No.	District or State.	Number of: Charges.	Number of: Circles.	Number of: Blocks.	Number of: Charge Superintendents.	Number of: Supervisors.	Number of: Enumerators.	Average number of houses per: Charge Superintendent.	Average number of houses per: Supervisor.	Average number of houses per: Enumerator.
	Total ..	*1,839*	*19,759*	*390,215*	*1,816*	*19,328*	*370,590*	*5,161*	*483*	*25*
1	Ganjam—									
	Synchronous	93	871	19,330	92	873	18,028	4,664	492	24
	Non-synchronous ..	16	154	3,779	16	154	1,262	5,062	526	64
2	Vizagapatam—									
	Synchronous	72	1,092	24,191	72	1,092	23,215	8,122	536	25
	Non-synchronous	134	470	6,304	134	117	773	1,886	2,151	327
3	Godavari, East—									
	Synchronous	51	730	13,604	51	730	13,558	6,495	467	26
	Non-synchronous	18	106	2,857	18	106	1,597	2,809	477	32
4	Godavari, West	45	516	9,341	45	516	9,272	5,175	461	24
5	Kistna	44	511	10,128	44	511	10,092	5,737	493	25
6	Guntur	73	831	17,212	73	831	17,005	5,705	501	24
7	Nellore	63	579	12,704	63	580	12,427	4,886	530	24
8	Cuddapah	54	398	8,644	54	398	8,681	3,657	496	23
9	Kurnool—									
	Synchronous	49	465	9,339	49	468	9,288	4,314	452	23
	Non-synchronous	3	13	69	3	13	61	348	80	17
10	Bellary	51	479	8,791	51	479	8,737	3,890	414	23
11	Anantapur	64	507	9,448	57	507	9,806	3,780	423	23
12	Madras	30	132	1,260	30	132	1,260	2,461	559	59
13	Chingleput	62	608	12,314	58	604	12,122	5,010	481	24
14	Chittoor—									
	Synchronous	59	571	12,143	59	571	11,610	4,639	479	24
	Non-synchronous	..	..	4	..	..	3	..	..	42
15	North Arcot	83	723	14,586	80	723	14,478	4,472	495	25
16	Salem	67	1,065	22,665	67	1,064	19,818	7,721	486	26
17	Coimbatore—									
	Synchronous	69	1,080	20,233	69	1,057	20,134	7,148	467	24
	Non-synchronous	1	5	401	1	5	311	3,446	686	11
18	South Arcot	71	935	17,928	71	932	17,902	6,271	478	25
19	Tanjore	80	1,018	19,941	78	1,020	18,526	6,249	477	26
20	Trichinopoly	63	849	16,283	63	849	16,213	6,254	464	24
21	Madura	67	866	16,594	67	863	16,297	5,976	464	25
22	Ramnad	96	818	17,603	94	818	16,502	3,978	458	22
23	Tinnevelly—									
	Synchronous	87	1,058	20,722	81	1,006	20,668	5,854	471	23
	Non-synchronous	1	3	46	1	3	46	1,145	381	25
24	The Nilgiris—									
	Synchronous	13	92	1,586	13	92	1,201	2,386	337	25
	Non-synchronous	4	18	336	4	18	383	2,248	499	27
25	Malabar—									
	Synchronous	90	1,338	25,615	90	1,338	25,710 }	6,303	422	23
	Non-synchronous	9	70	602	9	70	504 }			
26	South Kanara—									
	Synchronous	36	484	8,731	32	484	9,041	6,948	459	25
	Non-synchronous	..	44	1,114	..	44	891	..	501	25
27	Pudukkottai State	16	226	3,723	16	226	3,723	5,097	361	22
28	Banganapalle State	4	24	417	4	24	416	2,043	341	20
29	Sandur State	1	10	132	1	10	129	3,171	317	25

II.—Number of Forms supplied and used.

S. No.	District or State.	Enumeration Book covers (000) Supplied.	Enumeration Book covers (000) Used.	Block Lists (000) Supplied.	Block Lists (000) Used.	General schedules. Actual number (000) Supplied.	General schedules. Actual number (000) Used.	General schedules. Per 100 occupied houses. Supplied.	General schedules. Per 100 occupied houses. Used.	Other forms issued. House-hold schedules (actual).	Other forms issued. Boat Enumeration passes (actual).	Other forms issued. Travellers tickets. (00)
	Total—1921 ..	*422*	*418*	*394*	*386*	*5,039*	*4,854*	*81*	*59*	*17,560*	*4,183*	*5,168*
	Total—1931 ..	*536*	*495*	*546*	*503*	*6,157*	*5,891*	*65*	*64*	*10,489*	*3,265*	*4,606*
1	Ganjam—											
	Agency ..	2	2	2	2	27	26	33	32			
	Plains ..	25	24	25	24	309	300	72	69	446	20	45
2	Vizagapatam—											
	Agency ..	22	21	22	21	72	70	28	24			
	Plains ..	34	32	34	32	416	400	71	68	410	65	61
3	Godavari, East—											
	Agency ..	3	3	3	3	26	25	52	50			
	Plains ..	16	15	16	15	178	173	54	53	400	300	125
4	Godavari, West ..	10	9	9	8	93	89	40	38	216	..	119
5	Kistna ..	9	8	9	8	139	130	55	52	685	50	150
6	Guntur ..	27	26	27	25	206	200	49	48	556	45	218
7	Nellore ..	14	12	16	13	167	159	54	51	238	..	122
8	Cuddapah ..	10	9	11	10	112	110	58	55	190	..	56
9	Kurnool ..	10	9	11	10	122	119	53	56	76	..	129
10	Bellary ..	10	8	10	9	119	111	60	56	122	..	252
11	Anantapur ..	12	9	12	8	126	120	59	56	291	..	105
12	Madras ..	2	2	6	4	52	50	85	62	..	12	100
13	Chingleput ..	15	12	14	12	152	148	52	51	472	..	177
14	Chittoor ..	14	12	14	12	146	145	54	53	270	..	66
15	North Arcot ..	19	16	19	17	200	191	56	53	505	..	186
16	Salem ..	32	30	33	30	420	409	81	78	642	..	150
17	Coimbatore ..	31	30	31	30	425	408	88	83	613	35	186
18	South Arcot ..	31	30	31	30	420	411	84	80	338	40	251
19	Tanjore ..	33	30	32	31	408	401	79	76	313	740	352
20	Trichinopoly ..	19	17	19	17	271	262	68	65	509	..	302
21	Madura ..	24	22	25	22	262	259	67	62	517	100	332
22	Ramnad ..	20	19	20	19	252	250	60	59	245	..	52
23	Tinnevelly ..	30	29	31	29	413	417	82	81	451	120	195
24	Nilgiris ..	2	2	2	2	20	19	51	48	1,145	..	12
25	Malabar ..	38	37	39	38	352	350	56	55	552	1,170	529
26	South Kanara ..	18	16	18	16	180	172	61	55	174	578	214
27	Pudukkottai State	4	4	5	5	59	59	72	72	20	..	50
28	Banganapalle State	·5	·5	·5	·5	6	6	75	75	..	..	4
29	Sandur State ..	·2	·2	·2	·2	2	2	66	66	15	..	18

III.—District Census Charges.

S. No (1)	District. (2)	District office establishment. (3)	House numbering. (4)	Remuneration of census officers. (5)	Travelling allowance of census officers. (6)	Local purchase of stationery. (7)	Postage. (8)	Freight. (9)	Miscellaneous. Printing at Government presses. (10)	Miscellaneous. Printing at private presses. (11)	Miscellaneous. Miscellaneous. (12)	Total. (13)
		RS.	RS.	RS.	RS.	RS.	RS.	RS.	RS.	RS.	RS.	RS.
	1921 Total ..	*631*	*3,225*	*7,310*	*13,882*	*413*	*106*	*165*	*7,027*	*17,102*	*408*	*50,269*
	1931 Total ..	*4,394*	*1,924*	*1,142*	**1,38,664*	*432*	*1,042*	*230*	*16,869*	*13,907*	*1,458*	*1,31,980*
1	Ganjam ..	257	192	24	7,342	76	15	3	..	789	24	8,722
2	Vizagapatam ..	3,144	..	..	2,590	..	35	25	2,395	..	48	8,237
3	Godavari, East ..	190	13	..	7,655	24	58	77	..	770	81	8,868
4	Godavari, West ..	27	..	..	4,552	..	..	23	917	..	10	5,529
5	Kistna ..	..	..	..	4,025	..	..	11	850	..	70	4,956
6	Guntur ..	2	..	..	6,681	..	..	..	..	668	23	7,374
7	Nellore ..	..	..	..	4,538	..	..	..	..	2,432	25	6,995
8	Cuddapah ..	..	..	..	8,310	..	..	1	..	414	13	8,738
9	Kurnool ..	..	..	..	4,377	7	..	..	940	..	3	5,327
10	Bellary ..	..	..	..	2,688	..	..	..	777	..	14	3,479
11	Anantapur ..	..	..	..	3,484	1	10	5	..	675	1	4,176
12	Madras ..	774	1,719	1,113	2,694	307	37	..	..	216	578	7,438
13	Chingleput ..	..	..	..	6,126	..	..	2	1,430	..	18	7,582
14	Chittoor ..	..	..	..	4,883	..	..	4	1,920	..	11	6,818
15	North Arcot ..	..	..	..	7,277	..	5	5	..	260	66	7,613
16	Salem ..	..	..	..	8,337	..	10	24	1,161	..	18	9,550
17	Coimbatore ..	..	..	..	5,681	..	..	..	1,723	..	56	7,460
18	South Arcot ..	..	..	..	6,334	..	79	..	..	1,437	19	7,869
19	Tanjore ..	..	..	..	5,525	..	253	..	..	1,753	150	7,681
20	Trichinopoly ..	..	..	..	4,558	..	100	8	1,346	10	46	6,068
21	Madura ..	..	..	..	4,436	..	48	..	528	1,060	31	6,098
22	Ramnad ..	..	..	..	3,148	..	274	9	2,725	44	10	6,210
23	Tinnevelly ..	..	..	..	5,396	..	2	2	..	660	17	6,077
24	Nilgiris ..	..	..	..	3,547	..	..	..	151	..	..	3,698
25	Malabar ..	..	..	..	16,882	6	116	26	..	2,319	100	19,449
26	South Kanara ..	..	..	5	3,628	11	..	5	..	400	24	4,073

* Incomplete

CHAPTER II.

ABSTRACTION AND TABULATION.

THE 1921 system of copying and abstraction was continued, with some reluctance. I had hoped as will be seen from Chapter I, to use the village staff for enumeration and to pass thence to copying by the same agency, with district sorting offices. This had to be given up; the combination of circumstances in 1931 was too much. Unless conditions are equally adverse in 1941, however, the new system should be tried. The point is dealt with further at the end of this chapter.

Location of offices.

2. My object was to have offices situated in the areas with which they dealt and in particular to have Telugu abstraction done this time in the Telugu country. Practical considerations make some dispersion inevitable and Oriya, Kanarese and Malayalam abstraction have always had to be done in the respective linguistic areas, from the impossibility of recruiting sufficient competent men in Madras for these languages. Why Telugu abstraction was always done in Madras it is difficult to say. A further argument in favour of dispersion is the encouragement large concentrations give to the rise or spread of labour troubles. It needed no remarkable prescience to foresee these and it is better to have single offices in widely separated towns than large aggregations within one town, perhaps even under one roof. The final distribution was:

No.	Place.	Deputy Superintendent in charge.	Districts dealt with.
1	Berhampur ..	Khan Sahib Moinuddin Khan Sahib Bahadur, Revenue Divisional Officer, Chatrapur.	Ganjam and Vizagapatam (including Agencies).
2	Rajahmundry ..	M.R.Ry. S. Narayanaswami Nayudu Garu, Supervisor, Settlement Party No. I, Cocanada.	East Godavari (including Agency), West Godavari, Kistna and Guntur.
3	Bellary	M.R.Ry. P. V. Chelapathi Mudaliyar Avargal, Deputy Tahsildar, Cuddapah.	Anantapur, Bellary, Cuddapah, Kurnool, Banganapalle State, Nellore and Chittoor, except Kanarese books of Bellary and Tamil books of Chittoor.
4	Madras	M.R.Ry. R. Srinivasavarada Ayyangar Avargal, Inspecting Tahsildar, Madura.	Madras, Chingleput and the Nilgiris.
5	Tiruvannamalai.	M.R.Ry. S. Vrishabha Das Avargal, Deputy Tahsildar, Coimbatore.	Tamil books of Chittoor and all books of North Arcot, Salem and Coimbatore districts except Kanarese books of Coimbatore.
6	Cannanore ..	M.R.Ry. T. V. Ramunni Nayar Avargal, Deputy Tahsildar, Malabar.	Malabar, Anjengo and Tangasseri in Tinnevelly, and Malayalam books of South Kanara.
7	Mangalore ..	M.R.Ry. V. K. Sundaresha Sastri Avargal, Deputy Tahsildar, South Kanara.	South Kanara except Malayalam books, Sandur, Coorg, Kanarese books of Bellary and Coimbatore.
8	Tanjore I ..	M.R.Ry. T. K. Gopala Ayyar Avargal, Acting Head accountant, Nannilam.	South Arcot, Tanjore and Trichinopoly.
9	Tanjore II ..	M.R.Ry. M. C. George Avargal, Deputy Tahsildar, Salem.	Madura, Ramnad, and Tinnevelly except Anjengo and Tangasseri.

I could not get a convenient building in Madura, etc., for the south Tamil districts and had to accommodate that office in Tanjore; otherwise a distribution by region was achieved. The two offices in Tanjore were in different parts of the town.

3. The nature of the housing varied greatly. The Ganjam office was in the Haradakhandi Mutt at Berhampur. That town is the only place for this office, for nowhere else could sufficient Oriya staff be recruited. Accommodation was difficult to find however, and always will be for a full size office of 200 men; I was indebted to the courtesy of the Hindu Religious Endowment Board for allowing me the use of the mutt at a reasonable rent, and the fact that the trustee was an old acquaintance of my own Ganjam days helped to make things easier. It is likely that impending provincial changes will remove or greatly diminish any concern of the 1941 Superintendent with Oriya abstraction. The

Telugu delta office was at Rajahmundry, the heart of Andhradesa, in a large private bungalow. The rent was high and the proprietor exigent and disobliging but the only alternatives were Vizagapatam and Bellary, both unsuitable for various reasons, the former chiefly because of accommodation for office and staff, the latter because the Deccan office was already there and from considerations of recruitment: we could never have recruited 400 men in Bellary or got them to stay there. The Rajahmundry house made an excellent office in every way. The experiment of a census office in the Telugu Delta despite a difficult beginning proved a great success and if the system of large central offices has to be continued in 1941, one of them should be located there. I found in unexpected quarters and among the staff an appreciation of the departure which gave Andhradesa its own census offices and this circumstance was of some value when labour troubles threatened.

The Deccan office at Bellary was admirably housed in the old Station Hospital in the cantonment. Peculiar difficulties however attended this office as regards staff. The class of man recruitable was low and the leisurely Deccan habits take ill to matters requiring hustle.

Bellary, although rather beyond the actual Telugu area, is a suitable centre for a Telugu abstraction office and our experiment of 1931 worked out on the whole quite well. Sufficient Telugu staff for a full-sized office can be obtained and retained though with some difficulty. I do not think there would ever be any prospect of running a successful Kanarese office here however. If the central offices are continued in 1941, possible locations in Chittoor and Tirupati could be considered for one of the Telugu offices as alternatives to Bellary.

The other offices require little mention. No free buildings were available in Madras at the outset and all had to be hired: later on I was able to secure ample accommodation free of charge in buildings belonging to the Government of India formerly occupied by the Army Clothing Department. The Chatram at Tiruvannamalai made an excellent office in every way; I am indebted to Raja Sir Annamalai Chettiyar of Chettinad, through whose kindness we got this building free of rent.

Kanarese Office.

4. The Kanarese office will always be a problem of peculiar difficulty so long as central abstraction offices are continued. Madras Kanarese areas are in essence outlying fragments and possess all the attributes of outposts. Telugu influence is marked in Bellary Kanarese; Tamil affects Kollegal and Tulu Coondapoor. The areas are widely separated. Nowhere does a clear linguistic border run and only perhaps in the most westerly taluks of Bellary can one expect the entire schedules of a taluk to be in Kanarese. Kollegal will always have some Tamil books, the central taluks of Bellary will have both Telugu and Kanarese. An office located in Bellary will have great difficulty with the Kanarese written in Kollegal and cannot manage the Tamil books of that taluk. An office in Mangalore has difficulty with the Kanarese of both Bellary and Kollegal and cannot deal with either the Tamil or Telugu books.

Much the best place for a Kanarese central office would be Bangalore and since the office is comparatively small, accommodation could easily be found in the Civil and Military Station. It was my intention to have the office there this time but I gave up the idea as the Mysore Census Superintendent anticipated possible difficulties. After my experience of Mangalore and Mr. Boag's of Bellary in 1921, I am convinced however that in future any Kanarese central office should be in Bangalore. Prior consultation and constant liaison with the Mysore census authorities would avoid any difficulties in management, and the benefits would be considerable. In Bangalore men could be recruited able to read Tamil or Telugu as well as Kanarese and also the different varieties of Kanarese would be more readily interpreted. The entire books of certain taluks could be sent to this office for compilation of every table. This year I had to effect an interchange of slips between the Mangalore and the Tiruvannamalai and Bellary offices in order to secure complete taluk treatment for areas in which the original schedules were in more than one language.

Furniture.

5. Little could be borrowed this time. The University could spare nothing and the Commissioner for Government Examinations only 95 tables and 65 stools from 1st April 1931. As the Madras office began a month before that date furniture had to be hired in the interim. For other furniture competitive supply tenders were invited both in Madras and in the abstraction centres and the lowest tenders accepted, consideration being had to transit or other costs involved. The articles in question were tables (*a*), chairs (*b*), stools (*c*), racks (*d*), dealwood boxes (*e*), bamboo baskets (*f*) and pigeonholes for sorting (*g*). The table in the margin indicates to what extent local supply was used. Articles not specified were supplied from Madras.

Office.	Articles supplied locally.
Madras, Berhampur	All.
Rajahmundry, Tanjore	(*a*) to (*e*).
Cannanore	*d, e, f.*
Bellary	*d, e.*
Tiruvannamalai	*d.*
Mangalore	*e.*

Thus only Berhampur of the mufassal places could produce a tinsmith ready to knock up a couple of hundred sets of pigeonholes from old kerosene tins. A good deal depends on the energy of local officers in such matters. Ample intimation is given and if the tahsildar takes a timely interest local supply (which is to be preferred) should be possible at least in large towns. Pigeonholes cost Rs. 1–8–0 to Rs. 1–9–6 each. On these as on the deal boxes and racks there was a saving as compared with 1921, despite larger numbers required. Tables, chairs and stools had to be bought in much larger quantity and cost correspondingly more. The most interesting difference is in the cost of the bamboo baskets. These also were required in greater numbers but the much higher cost is mainly a reflection of greater general expensiveness of bamboo. The table in the margin gives details of supply and cost.

Article.	Number.	Cost. RS.
Tables	1,888	6,945
Chairs	80	210
Stools	1,843	3,080
Racks	43	440
Boxes	277	1,760
Baskets	3,355	1,760
Pigeonholes	1,742	2,570

Rs. 4,097 was realized by the sale of these articles at the close of the operations. Periodical reports are required from Collectors during the preliminary year on the progress of enumeration preparations. I would suggest regular periodical reports also on the progress of arrangements entrusted or referred to them which bear on the location, equipment and recruitment of abstraction offices. The existence of a prescribed periodical return serves as a useful reminder. An attitude not uncommon where such matters are concerned is 'mañana' and where district offices are busy and the critical date distant one can see how such an attitude may arise. Actually, however, it is important to know as early as possible to what extent local supply will operate.

Stationery.

6. The appendix at the end shows the stationery used by the various offices. Unused stock was sold by public auction and Rs. 364 realized.

Superintendence.

7. I had great difficulty in obtaining suitable men for the headship of the abstraction offices. The main cause was a ruling of the Madras Government that service as a Deputy Superintendent of Census could not be allowed to count towards the period of qualifying service required for certain posts. Now the type best suited for a Deputy Superintendent, namely the young, ambitious man wishful to be a Deputy Collector in due course, is almost invariably acting or about to act as Deputy Tahsildar or Tahsildar. If he takes up the post of Deputy Superintendent it may mean that while he is so employed some junior gets in to act and therefore automatically gets in front of him in the promotion race. No man could be expected to go against his own interests and the position was made clear to every possible appointee. In many ways the post of a Deputy Superintendent of Census is eminently suitable for testing the qualifications of a rising public servant. He has to assimilate new work quickly, he has to control a staff of one or two hundred men who are almost certain to try to spin out work if not to give more overt trouble. He has to keep up a steady flow of work and to arrange the functioning of his office so that no man is ever sitting idle while another is overwhelmed. A census abstraction office has

copying, sorting and compilation running in parallel and in series practically throughout; the staff varies in quality and the work in difficulty; to secure freedom alike from congestion and gaps needs discrimination, vision, and unremitting attention in the man at the head. The post is in fact a severe test of general capacity and might well be admitted to count for qualifying service up to a maximum of six months.

When the difficulties were made known to the Madras Government they declared themselves prepared to consider the issue of a special order if in any case the effect of an officer's period as Deputy Superintendent was that he completed his term of probation for Revenue Subordinate Service after another officer who otherwise would have been later than him. Individual officers were therefore protected. The Government maintained however their attitude that service as Deputy Superintendent should not be deemed to be or allowed to count as service qualifying for the post of tahsildar. Actually the Board of Revenue was throughout considerate and helpful and to Mr. MacEwen, its secretary, I am indebted for much help and counsel. The Madras Government too relaxed its ruling slightly to enable me to have the services of Khan Sahib Moinuddin for Berhampur. The general effect of the ruling however was that the type of man wanted fought shy of the post despite considerable offered increase in pay, and though in the end I recruited quite a sound team (one or two were excellent), it was only after much difficulty.

I recommend that in 1941 an agreement be made beforehand with the Madras Government that service up to six months as head of an abstraction office, certified as satisfactory by the Superintendent, be counted towards qualifying service for tahsildar or deputy tahsildar. It is important to have this declaration out beforehand so that prospective appointees will know in advance exactly where they stand.

Training.

8. Previous practice in training the abstraction staff was to bring all supervisors into Madras for a class in which they acted as copyists and the deputy superintendents as checkers and supervisors. I departed from this and conducted a class which comprised the nine deputy superintendents and some Madras supervisors. Every man (including myself) began at the very beginning and copied several hundred slips from representative schedules of Madras city. Thereafter we worked through the various tables. Deputy superintendents were then sent out to open their offices and train their own supervisors. Recruitment of these last was so arranged that every office had one or two men with previous experience in a census abstraction office. The departure was successful and the saving in pay and travelling allowance of supervisors appreciable. Deputy superintendents must inevitably exercise full responsibility later on and it seemed worthwhile to concentrate on them and ensure their familiarity with every process and leave them to train their own men. Their procedure in training their men followed the general lines of the original class; the supervisors began by copying each a considerable number of entries; these were checked, passed and in due course sorted. Meanwhile the deputy superintendent in addition to supervising their training had been recruiting his abstractors and generally preparing for the full opening of the office. Supervisors with previous experience or quicker intelligence picked up the work sooner and to such, as they became qualified, were entrusted the first batches of abstractors. These in their turn were trained in copying and the office came thus gradually into full swing.

Recruitment of abstractors.

9. As indicated above, deputy superintendents were, apart from a few appointments made by myself of personal applicants, left to appoint their own abstractors subject to certain general rules. Among these last was that a definite writing test should be applied, for a clumsy or flowery or otherwise illegible hand is the last thing to be desired in a copyist. Ability to write quickly was demanded: not all officers realized that there are definite variations in physical capacity for quick writing. Abstraction being on an outturn basis, the necessity for physical equipment is obvious; besides, a quick pen and a quick mind go often together. Every office had to include representatives of all districts dealt with and the principal sections of the population by religion, community and mothertongue.

The delegation to deputy superintendents of the selection of their copyists was deliberate. I wished there to be the fullest degree of self-confidence and sense of responsibility and to leave as much as possible to their discretion. The constitution of these abstraction offices, temporary men recruited for urgent work on piece rates, almost invites labour trouble; they are situated far apart and the officers-in-charge must be prepared to act on their own initiative and judgment; all the more reason for leaving these last as free a hand as possible. All this was explained to the deputy superintendents before they set forth; they were told that while the Superintendent could always be invoked in case of need, they must look upon such appeal as a last instead of a first resort. Thus when the strike in the Madras office occurred when I was far away from Madras, I did not return on the spot but held myself ready to do so should my intervention prove unavoidable. It did not; the deputy superintendent dealt with the difficulty himself, greatly to the benefit of discipline in his office.

On the whole, deputy superintendents chose wisely. Tiruvannamalai had the largest proportion of students and senior schoolboys; this office achieved regularly the best copying outturns. Berhampur recruited a surprising number of well qualified men and the same applied to all the other offices except Bellary and Mangalore. Not that educated unemployed are not present in the last named place; only they seem to need or desire employment less. Well controlled, the schoolboy/student type makes the best copyist. Older men are on the whole better sorters.

Supervisors were recruited from permanent Government servants and were given, like other officers deputed to census duty, a pay increase of 20 per cent. It was not always easy to get good men for, as in the case of deputy superintendents, there seemed to be a fear that census duty might interfere with prospects. Too many volunteers were such as their districts would be glad to lose. The supervisor is an important person in a census abstraction office and I would suggest that if central offices are continued in 1941 a higher maximum pay be fixed; this might induce more revenue inspectors, the best material for supervisors, to come forward. If the suggestion for district sorting is given effect to, the problem in this form will not arise.

Payment of abstractors. 10. There is no escaping the necessity for payment to be on a piecetime basis. Speed is essential though it must attend upon accuracy. The interests of a temporary staff will generally be towards prolongation of their employment, the exact opposite of what we seek, speedy conclusion of abstraction and compilation activities. To recruit on a mere monthly wage would mean inevitably prolonging greatly the time required unless drastic recourse were made to fines; and such a result would be in essence a return to piecework. Thus while for the purpose of budgeting and general calculation Rs. 25 a month was taken as an abstractor's pay, he was really paid on a pure piecework system, one rupee a day for a certain prescribed outturn. This rate, considering that the work required no particular degree of intelligence or education and considering the state of the labour market, was eminently reasonable. The outturns were fixed partly from the experience of 1921 and partly from the results of my own class held before the opening of the abstraction offices. For the first six days no outturn was prescribed. This is fair and also advisable; copying is largely automatic and inevitably so in its middle and later stages. Therefore the desideratum is to fix in the copyists' minds at the beginning the correct principles and exemplars. If they are not concerned with outturn considerations, they are much more likely to learn thoroughly the points of importance. Following upon this first trial week an outturn of 512 slips a day was required for the standard pay. Outturn in excess of this was rewarded at the rate of one anna for every 32 slips. Deductions were at the rate of 8 slips for every error. My reason in fixing these was to achieve easy calculation by adhering to multiples of 8 or 16. After a month the outturn was raised to 640 per day. Several offices, notably Berhampur, Bellary and Rajahmundry, protested against these outturns. These three offices, particularly Bellary, had a poorer quality of men and had had certain other difficulties, and after personal inspection I allowed the training period to continue for one week more and after that enforced the ordinary outturns. To say that these outturns were excessive is ridiculous. I myself with no experience of continuous high-speed writing, found myself copying 130 slips in an hour, the second day of doing the work. What is required is concentration more than anything else ; it is possibly because concentration is a rare virtue and rarest of all among the type of men who come to census offices for employment that complaints arose. How eminently reasonable the outturns were, is illustrated by the fact that Ramachandran of the Tiruvannamalai office copied in one day over 2,200 slips. It is true that he was a particularly smart youth and that he worked more than 8 hours but he did not work more than 9 ; all that happened on the particular day was that he took a very short time for his tiffin and returned to work. The outturns were facilitated by the extensive use made of ticks (✓) and contractions. 'V' and 'S' on Hindu slips were sufficient for Vaishnavite or Saivite, while 'S' on a Muslim slip meant Sunni, 'R.C.' on a Christian slip was sufficient for Roman Catholic and so on. Far from saying that these outturns are excessive I would definitely suggest that if the same type of men is used in 1941 the copying outturns could be raised. The final sorting rates applied this time given below * represented probably a fairly close approximation to reasonable possibility.

* Table.		Number of slips.	
VI	Birthplace	15,000	Cities.
		20,000	Rural.
VII	Age, sex and civil condition by religion	4,800	
VIII	Civil condition by age for selected castes	8,000	
IX	Infirmities	16,000	
X	Occupation	4,000	
XII	Unemployment of educated persons	6,000	
XIII	Literacy by religion and age	9,000	Males.
		15,000	Females.
XIV	Literacy by selected castes	12,000	Males.
		16,000	Females.
XV	Part I. Mothertongue	16,000	
	Part II. Subsidiary language	12,000	
XVII	Race, tribe and caste	8,000	
XIX	Europeans, etc., by race and age	8,000	

Some men worked during the no-outturn stage and then left. Deputy superintendents quite rightly demurred to giving these men the full pay. The orders I gave were : this concession of no-outturn was definitely given with a view to using towards future activity the training acquired in the no-outturn period. Where a man proposed to leave before entering on the outturn period at all he could not claim this concession and should be paid for his period of work purely on the outturn basis, that is to say, the number of slips he had copied minus deductions for errors should be divided by the fixed outturn and the result in rupees paid to him.

11. The intimation of a 10 per cent cut in the census budget following upon a heavy cut previously made by the Census Commissioner himself made economies essential. These were mainly secured by the abandonment of certain tables and enhancement of outturns. The intimation made me decide upon a further raising of the copying outturn to 720 slips per day and the elevation of nearly all sorting rates. This was resented in most offices but I remained firm and the trouble died away. It is not unreasonable that a staff paid by outturns should object to the raising of the standard ; what the staff failed to realize was that in copying, facility grows so quickly that the raising of the standards merely tends to restore remuneration to the originally contracted basis. This budget cut created a very difficult position. Census budgets do not lend themselves to much modification without affecting the work to be done. They are not like budgets covering engineering or construction works which can at need be postponed. My budget was very closely calculated on strengths, outturns and reasonable payments and to make a percentage cut on such a budget resulted in some work having to be abandoned. In the result, several tables were left out altogether while others were considerably simplified. I had already secured the Madras Government's consent to abolish the rather preposterous table of infirmity by selected castes and two others for occupation by caste, tribe or race. The Government of India ordered the abolition of three tables in addition to these and the modification of four others. Not all those contractions of the work and of the statistics are to be deplored. Infirmity by castes, e.g., has never appeared to me worth publishing.

Village statistics.

12. A suggestion was also made that the village statistics should not be extracted at all by the census staff but that the documents should be handed over to district or municipal authorities for them to extract what figures they desired. This contraction of census effort is to be deprecated. For one thing, the village statistics are much more valuable than some of the pretentious Imperial Tables and much more frequently consulted. One of my ambitions at this census was to make these village statistics fuller and more useful. On the other hand, given the attitude of the Provincial Government that everything bearing the census ticket should be an Imperial charge, it was but logical for the Central Government to say 'village statistics are not ours; why should we extract them?'. I proposed to the Census Commissioner and the Madras Government that the local Government should bear the cost of extraction. To have them compiled by district staff from census papers would be a retrograde step. For one thing, in this presidency, no village register is drawn up. It has never been the practice to do so. Totals are struck direct from the sorter's tickets and transferred then and there to the village statistics sheet. The census staff are skilled and experienced in tabulation and compilation; they understand the tickets and other census forms they use. Their work is speedier and more accurate. To expect these figures be drawn up as a sideline activity in every Collector's office and municipality and reach any real degree of accuracy or trustworthiness, is to cherish an illusion. Collectors in Madras have too many activities as it is to control and it is certain that presuming the local Government wished up-to-date village statistics—and it is difficult to imagine them not so wishing—they would have to employ extra staff in every district and municipality for the purpose of compiling these village and ward figures. In other words, they would probably find that far from having saved money they had paid more to achieve less. The Madras Government accepted these arguments and bore the cost of extraction.

The village statistics are of great use in compilation work; they were the means of bringing to light certain district errors in fixing of town boundaries and so enabling Imperial Tables I, IV and V to be brought into accord with facts. These village statistics should be completed as soon as possible, adequate staff being appointed from the first to keep their compilation going *pari passu* with the completion of Sorters' ticket I.

Copying and sorting procedure.

13. The principles of the copying and sorting system have been set out in previous reports, notably 1901, and need not be detailed again. 1921 experience was taken as guide and departures from it were slight. No special stamper was employed for entering the block and other identifying numbers on the slips. Each copyist entered these in a fixed order, charge-circle-block, on the top of the slip, with also a taluk indication. Initial letters or contractions were used for taluk names. It seems desirable that responsibility for a slip should be absolute and the identifying numbers are important details. The copyist was given no allowance of time to cover this numbering and thus the cost of the stamper and his stamp was saved. The symbols on the slips were altered in order to make male and female more immediately distinguishable; the anthropological symbols hitherto used are not beyond risk of confusion for the hurried and inexpert. Slips therefore bore a bold triangle or circle to indicate sex. For civil condition, the sex symbol left blank indicated unmarried; a single line in the centre of it showed married and a cross widowed. There was an element of the appropriate in the development of these three symbols which made instruction and comprehension easy. It is important to include, if possible, in a system of symbols, elements which will appeal to the minds of the type of person who is to apply them. These symbols were explained thus: every one is young and has a period free from family cares—that freedom is appropriately indicated by leaving the sex symbol blank; marriage means an invasion of that freedom—indicate it therefore by a line or tick; widowhood means the second stage too has passed—therefore cross out the line representing it, i.e., make a X. In practice the entry of a wrong symbol for civil condition was the rarest of mistakes.

14. Free use was made of contractions but no unauthorized ones were permitted. Before a district was taken up, contractions for its taluk names were drawn up ; usually they coincided with the contractions used in the Madras revenue administration. B was allowed for Brahman, A.D. for Adi-Dravida, A.A. for Adi-Andhra, but no other contractions for caste names were tolerated. Only for the standard agricultural occupations were contractions allowed. I would recommend an extension of the use of prescribed contractions and the beginning of their use in the enumeration stage. There is no reason why the enumerator should not indicate birth in the district of enumeration by a tick or ability to read and write by the same symbol. Every answer which = 'Yes' should from the beginning be represented by a tick and every answer which = 'No' by a dash. Approved contractions could be drawn up for the 26 Madras districts which cover over 90 per cent of the birthplace entries. The main religions could be indicated by H, M and X, civil condition by U, M, W. Contractions at the enumeration stage are inadvisable for caste or occupation save that for the standard cultivation heads, cultivating owner, cultivating tenant, etc., C.O., C.T., etc., might be prescribed in all districts. This would save trouble in the abstraction offices later on and would obviate risk of confusion between different vernacular phrases actually meaning the same. **Contractions.**

It may be argued that the approval of contractions at the enumeration stage must lead to error. Not necessarily at all if the contractions are carefully drawn up and are uniform throughout. They could be printed easily on every enumeration book cover and in the manual of instructions and I am certain would be more readily seized by the average enumerator's mind than the traditional descriptive paragraphs about each column. In any case mere practice would speedily teach him. The benefits to him would be much less writing and to the compilation office far clearer schedules and more uniform data. Where supplementary detail is given, e.g., of religious sect, the enumerator would be able to accommodate it easily and clearly within the column. The schedule entry to be at its best and clearest is like a picture : it needs framing. That framing is secured by having blank space all round it. Hence the desirability of brevity.

It may be argued—and was in fact argued in one of my abstraction offices—that contractions should not be in English characters but in vernacular. This view seems to me to miss one essential point. The use of English characters or of such a symbol as a tick or dash has great merit from the very fact of it being completely dissociated from the vernacular, a point of particular importance in bilingual areas ; it will be more carefully learnt and used and confusion is avoided. An illiterate bus driver may not be able to read the word 'danger' but the red triangle conveys an immediate and effective message. Any one who can write at all can learn to make a particular kind of mark.

I would recommend that at least in Madras a systematic scheme of contractions be drawn up early in 1940 on the above lines and embodied in the manual, schedules and training. If my suggestion to use only village officers in enumeration is carried out, I should be inclined to suggest even an extension of contractions into the larger caste names, certainly Brahman, Adi-Dravida, Adi-Andhra. I encouraged the use of certain contractions during my enumeration tours and wish I had laid them down from the beginning. It is essential that contractions be uniform, i.e., in practice that they be laid down by the superintendent ; this secured there is little fear of abuse in practice and it is time a serious effort was made to reduce the enumerator's scriptory labour.

15. As in 1921 separate infirmity slips were written immediately after the ordinary slip for the item. 1921 experience was also followed in running Sorter's Ticket I *pari passu* with copying. This needs careful control by deputy superintendent and supervisors however if it is to be a success. Three sorters may not be able to keep pace with 17 copyists ; it depends on the capacities of the individuals and on the outturns in force. Generally speaking, only a really good supervisor will manage this well ; in the hands of a second rate man it may lead to confusion and instead of detecting copying errors will introduce **Sorter's ticket I, etc.**

other error of its own. I devoted considerable attention to this item in my inspection of the abstraction offices and was not satisfied with the result and as a consequence had the sorting transferred to a separate section under a chosen supervisor. This, I think, is the better course. It secures the end of having Ticket I done quickly and yet achieves concentration of effort and supervision. Most men of the class from which our supervisors are drawn prefer to have only one clear task at a time and it is well to consider their idiosyncrasy. A further difficulty of the original system lay in the occasional absence of a sorting clerk. The copying went on as before but the sorting branch was shorthanded and any man allocated had not the skill of his predecessor and resented being put on to work where his copying celerity was of no avail to earn him extra money.

Slips were kept separate by sex and religion throughout and men handled the same religion throughout. Distribution by sorter's unit was continued and as in 1921 was found satisfactory and lent itself well to subsidiary enquiries. The closeness of control and check it requires were found well within the competence of the supervising staff. Specially competent supervisors and sections were evolved in the course of the earlier operations and to these were given work of more than usual difficulty, e.g., large towns and occupations. This specialization is of much value and should be introduced wherever possible. It is particularly useful in occupation sorting and as this comes towards the end of the operations selection of the best personnel has become possible. Owing to retrenchment the caste sorting was a comparatively minor item this time. Perhaps it will have vanished altogether by 1941.

Diaries and special returns. 16. Deputy superintendents were directed to keep a diary and to enter in it day by day any matter bearing on their office and its work. The diaries varied in value but some were full and interesting and had obviously been of value to the writers themselves, the statement of problems having helped them to a better realization and decision on methods and solution. I recommend future prescription of such diaries.

Deputy superintendents were encouraged to make local enquiries on their own initiative whenever wide or peculiar and not readily accountable differences or variations in taluk or municipal or village behaviour became apparent. They were told to make their figures as informative as possible and not to hesitate to supply illustrative or explanatory comment. These instructions applied also to rare terms encountered in the course of copying. Lists of these were kept and local enquiries instituted.

Principles of check. 17. I found that check tended to be too rarely informed by judgment. Supervisors especially were content to go by routine. Random selection of slips for check is essential in the sense that the copyist or sorter should never know beforehand which actual items will be chosen ; it does not mean that the person checking should follow no principle but chance. An engineer in testing devotes particular attention to points of strain and therefore more likely weakness ; so in checking copying or sorting the points where error is more likely to enter should be observed or excogitated and particular attention paid to them. Thus in copying, any point of change after a long sequence of identical entries is a fruitful source of error, for mere momentum, if one may use the phrase, might well carry over the term become familiar. Specific instruction should be given in this to all supervisors.

The entry in the slips of full enumeration detail for occupation is essential. Copyists were apt to cut this down in copying in order to increase outturn. This should be a test point ; where in the schedule considerable occupation detail is given, choose that slip for check. Such mutilation of occupation entries may lead to great difficulty in the sorting stages and should be drastically punished. Check of receipt of enumeration schedules should be not by invoices but by circle lists, i.e., not by what is actually sent but by what should have been sent. A deputy superintendent should not be satisfied till he has accounted for every block shown in every circle list. Omission to check by circle lists led in one abstraction office to the delayed despatch of certain military schedules not being observed.

No administrative circumstance affecting the tables should be left unverified. One deputy superintendent assumed that town and village boundaries of 1921 would be unaltered in 1931, another that taluk areas are unchanging. Nothing should be exempt from census verification. The collection of fresh facts of population is a suitable occasion for testing the validity of other details.

18. There was some avoidable excess in the indents for slips, Berhampur and Cannanore being the chief offenders. A lack of consideration and failure to use available data were the causes of the excess in this as in the excessive indents for schedules discussed in Chapter I. The provisional enumeration results give quite a close enough indication of the number of slips that will actually be required and modifications of the supply made by the superintendent should be comparatively slight. Great excess or defect is impossible. Prior instructions were given on this to deputy superintendents but did not prevent free and unnecessary recourse by one or two to the telegraph. **Indents for slips.**

19. A small point which may seem too obvious to need stating but which I found to be very generally not realized is the importance of having all figures of similar value, units, tens, etc., in a true vertical line. Men should be trained to do this and one source of difficulty, delay and error is removed. Sorter's tickets and compilation registers might well be provided with faint vertical lines to facilitate columnar tabulation.

20. This followed the general scheme of previous censuses and so long as large central offices are maintained it will differ little in essentials. An important point is to ensure that compilation of the tables corresponding to I to V of the 1931 list should be done *pari passu* with sorting. I found this the weakest point of the work of my abstraction offices and would suggest that at instruction classes in future practice be given in it. Actual census details will not be available but the system can be practised. If mother-tongue detail is to be put in the village statistics these of course cannot be released until the language tables are finally prepared. They should, however, be ready in all other respects as soon as possible because they are of great assistance in checking other tables and in the general work of the compilation office. It was through the use of the village statistics that I was enabled this year to detect inaccuracies in the work of one or two districts in preparing their census divisions and in fact to detect the complete omission of one small village in Ramnad. Each abstraction office should have sufficient men to keep pace completely with the sorting work. I found this year with the increased outturns that deputy superintendents were inclined not to keep up the strength of their compilation sections in proportion and the central office had a certain amount of extra work in consequence. **Compilation.**

21. A good deal of preliminary work can be done in the preparation year. Tahsildars should be asked to go over the village statistics of the previous census and indicate any alterations in village or town boundaries, numbers, etc., and to bring up to date the general information introduced at this census. Their particular attention should be invited to (1) the need for distinguishing homonymous villages uniformly by giving the nearest important village, (2) indicating prominently villages actually uninhabited in 1940–41. Villages uninhabited in 1931 may not be so in 1941 and vice versa. (3) The villages or portions of villages which fall within the bounds of a census town should be clearly shown. **Preliminary work.**

Every tahsildar should be asked to send to the superintendent two copies of the 1931 village statistics for his taluk corrected up to date on the above lines. These should be scrutinized in the superintendent's office and one copy handed over to the abstraction officers concerned when they assemble for the preliminary training.

Tahsildars should also be directed to distinguish in their circle lists between homonymous villages by the same detail as they give in the corrected village statistics referred to above. This will facilitate abstraction operations and check.

All this can be completed before abstraction or compilation starts. Similarly for subsidiary tables not depending on census results and other general information; much can be done in the preliminary year. I would suggest early issue of the cross-check instructions so that these can be used in the instruction class which precedes the opening of abstraction. I found that deputy superintendents grasped the check principles fairly well but it would be useful to have these well in advance so that they can be thoroughly studied and applied.

Units.

22. In all compilation except for complicated tables like caste and occupation, and certainly for mothertongue, sex, civil condition and literacy, taluk and municipality should be kept separate throughout. Where any particular enquiry is in contemplation totals could be taken by charge for the table concerned. Taluk detail is always useful and involves little extra work. The taluk in some ways is the real administrative unit and must always be in a province where districts run into thousands of square miles.

Cross-check principles.

23. The compilation unit for the village statistics is the village or town based on the block.

For the provincial tables it is the taluk, based on the village or town.

For the imperial tables it is the district based on the taluk.

For subsidiary tables it is the natural division, based on the district.

The above statement indicates the lines check and preparation should follow. Instructions for cross-check should be drafted carefully and concisely and distributed to all supervisors, who should be trained in their application. One class of table leads to another and various columns in one should be reproduced in others and so on.

24. If my suggestions for copying and sorting on a district basis are accepted no essential change is involved in compilation procedure. Each district office should do compilation of the tables for its district and should complete the village statistics also, further compilation being done in the central office. For this work men of good qualifications should be employed. Karnams will do for the copying and sorting but it would be better to employ experienced clerks on some extra remuneration for compilation. Compilers this year as in previous years were recruited like the ordinary temporary census staff. I should be inclined, however, to recruit these men from permanent Government servants on a pay definitely above that of the other census workers. Their work requires a sense of system and method and some office experience which cannot ordinarily be found in the type of man recuited temporarily.

Natural divisions.

25. I had thought this year of preparing subsidiary tables for regions more 'natural' than the hitherto accepted natural divisions. Retrenchment intervened, but I would suggest that consideration be given to this and that figures be taken out for areas more truly associated than, *e.g.*, Nellore with the Circars or Chittoor with East Coast Central. The taluk would have to be taken as unit but this can easily be done and the taluk should really be the compilation unit in any case. Figures for the present natural divisions would have to be extracted also for continuity with previous censuses.

Linguistic area tables.

26. A departure this year was to prepare compendium tables for the linguistic divisions of the presidency. These will be found as an appendix to the report. I recommend the continuation of this and the inclusion of perhaps even more detail. This matter of linguistic separation has attracted much attention and is likely to attract more in the ensuing decade and the desirability of giving some census illustration to it is obvious. The census tables and report should try to reflect particular problems of the time. It may be of course that linguistic provinces will have come into being by the time the 1941 census arrives; then the suggested tables would be otiose. Possibly however a complete linguistic separation is unlikely.

Village statistics. Changes.

27. The village statements saw considerable development at this census. These are in many ways the most useful and certainly the most often-used of census productions and should be designed to serve as closly as possible the

convenience of the district officers who have to consult them. An officer arriving in a district with which he is unacquainted should have among his standard references something which will show him in compendious form the chief circumstances of the area under his charge. For example, if more than one mothertongue prevails it would be an obvious convenience if details of its distribution were at hand. Information of the chief markets, the chief sources of industry or peculiar activities and the chief centres where festival aggregations may be expected, with the dates for these last—all are items of information of obvious value.

The old form of village statistics contained totals for sexes and for Hindus, Muslims, Christians and other religions. Uninhabited villages were shown by an asterisk. The first improvement made at this census was to show the composition of the Hindu community. Village statistics should reflect as much as possible the main themes and circumstances of administration. The position of the depressed classes, their numbers and distribution, had been attracting steadily more attention and with the advent of panchayat boards and community representation on them, were achieving more and more importance. For every village therefore Hindus are shown under Brahmans, depressed classes and others. Appreciation of the value of this separation was shown by the department concerned with panchayats constantly consulting these village statements in the proof stage or earlier.

Tahsildars were asked to give information relating to chief festival centres with the nature of the festival and the date, markets, prominent industries and other items of importance in the life of the taluk.

An abiding obscurity in the village statistics was the homonymous village. Where differentiation was given at all the practice had been to add the survey number. Theoretically this was an excellent distinction. Practically it was not of much use because very few people consulting the village statistics would have a list of villages immediately at hand or what is still more important, a plan to show where the various survey numbers lay. Latitude and longitude is a possible means of differentiation of greater practical use ; this again however requires a map for its full application. Simple terms like east, west, north and south, are better and best of all is the name of the nearest town or large village. It was this last mode which was impressed upon taluk officers. Not all responded, but preferred to give other indicative terms. I would suggest for 1941 an insistence upon orientation by means of local references. The Tamil districts are the most prolific in homonymous villages, Kovilpatti in Tinnevelly and most taluks of Ramnad being the worst offenders.

Details were given of the composition of the elements of floating population. It is often important and useful to know how the floating element is made up. For example the specification of the strangers in Kovvur taluk who had come for the sweet toddy season will prevent any misconception of the nature of the additions to the village populations occasioned.

Mothertongue detail.

28. Possibly the most important departure was in the indication of mothertongue constitution. In connection with the impending formation of an Oriya Boundary Committee, I arranged for mothertongue detail to be extracted by villages in the five critical plains taluks of Ganjam. This detail is embodied in the village statistics. Elsewhere village extraction on this scale could not be undertaken on grounds of expense but I was loth to let the statistics go out without illustration of one of the province's most marked characteristics and a matter of prime importance to administrators, the many language frontiers. In every abstraction office therefore, when once village populations were known the enumeration schedules were taken up in turn. A clerk ran his eye down the mothertongue column, adding up as he went the returns of any mothertongue other than that already determined as the prevailing one of the taluk. If its total for the village equalled or exceeded 10% of the village population he extracted the percentage and it was entered in the statistics. If less than 10% no action was taken. Ten per cent was fixed on for two reasons : (i) it was a proportion requiring no calculation, as a mere glance at the village population

gave 10% also by a shift of the decimal point; (ii) it was the lowest percentage that could be said to represent an appreciable element of the village population justifying extraction and presentation in the statistics and also eliminated waste of time on inconsiderable elements which in many cases would come from casual strangers and not indicate abiding village features at all. No exotic mothertongues were considered; Bengali, Gujarati, etc., even supposing they had anywhere reached 10% were not counted. To economise effort was one reason; another and chief was that our object was to represent genuine regional conditions, not fortuitous aggregations. There was no ban against non-presidency languages as such: Marathi and Konkani in Kanara, Lambadi in the Deccan and Hindustani passim are effectively presidency mothertongues and consequently considered for village representation. Where the prevailing mothertongue was not beyond doubt, figures for the chief contenders were taken out. In some taluks where the predominance of one mothertongue was overwhelming, no attempt was made to take out village figures. The Telugu delta districts came within this category.

29. In the published statistics the prevailing mothertongue is given on the flyleaf of each taluk section and percentages of 10% or above shown against the villages only for other mothertongues. This secures economy in print and neatness. Where there were rivals for the prevalence or effective competition, taluk percentages for all were given on the flyleaf, one was adopted as prevailing, and village percentages given for the others. The Deputy Superintendent in charge of Salem, Coimbatore and North Arcot took out percentages of 10 or above for all mothertongues and his figures were published. The officer in charge of Kanara chose more than one prevailing language and took village figures only for the others with the result that the information is rather less full in that district than elsewhere, unfortunately, for Kanara is the presidency's most polyglot area except for Vizagapatam Agency. On the whole, however deputy superintendents took much interest in this development of the village statistics and I am indebted to them for their efforts.

Agency statistics.

30. Separate village statistics are not given in the Agency for the great majority of villages. This was the established Madras practice which had its origin in the fact that the Agency village bears no resemblance to that of the plains, but is a mere collection of a few houses not always even permanent in site. The number of such villages ran into hundreds and to print separate village details would have meant an extra expenditure approaching Rs. 1,000. The Madras Government saw no reason to depart from the previous practice of clubbing villages and this was in consequence maintained. In many ways it would be interesting to have individual village details for the Agency; in particular this would be useful from a mothertongue and tribe point of view. On the whole, however, I would suggest in future Agency village statistics that the Mutta be taken as the unit where the system exists as it does in Ganjam Agency. This unit of quasi-paternal jurisdiction is in many ways the true unit of at least the Kond Agency and figures grouped by it would have illustrative and other value.

31. I would advise strongly that the inclusion in village statistics of general local detail be continued at future censuses. Mothertongue reference is also useful but involves a good deal of extra scrutiny and check. Generally speaking, if any particular administrative problem is present at the time of the next census, consideration should be had to the possibility of illustrating it, or some aspects of it, in these village statistics.

Machine tabulation.

32. Machine tabulation was turned down for this census on the ground of expense. It is likely that in 1941 too economy will be on the side of the present system, particularly if full use is made of the advantages the Madras revenue system offers to the census. An estimate for machine extraction of this year's tables was almost twice the actual cost of the other method and so long as a gap of such dimensions exists mechanical methods hardly deserve consideration. The chief advantage of these methods is the avoidance of large staffs and the fact that the cards once punched contain every census detail from which any combination desired but not previously taken out in printed tables can at any

time be produced merely by sending the cards through a machine. With growing complexity of administration this last advantage will tend to grow in importance. The advantage is with the present methods. Mechanical methods are advantageous where clerical labour and office accommodation and equipment are alike expensive ; where labour is cheap and efficient and working conditions simpler the machine brings no advantage to compensate for the greatly increased expense. It seems however that if some of the detail hitherto recorded at Indian censuses (e.g., district birthplace, caste) is given up it should be possible to condense the columns into half a card or less and so considerably reduce one of the chief contributions to the expense.

If machine tabulation were to be introduced it would be necessary to remodel the enumeration schedule to suit the card, and a coding column would be required after each column in the schedule. In other words, the decision on tabulation would have to precede the casting of the schedule form. All this implies prolonged investigation and consideration and it is one of the disadvantages attendant on the phœnix-like succession of the Indian census that lengthy preliminary processes and experiment are difficult if not impossible ; countries with some form of permanent bureau such as the United States are much better situated from this point of view.

APPENDIX.

Serial number.	List of stationery articles.	Unit.	Quantity supplied.	Quantity used.
1	Cloth—			
	(a) Grey domestic, 30″, local	Yard ..	240	121½
	(b) Wax, in pieces of 5 yards by 1 yard, local.	Piece ..	2	....
2	Envelopes: Manilla—			
	(a) S.E. 6. 11″ × 4½″, local	Number ..	6,250	5,680
	(b) S.E. 7. 16″ × 6″, local	Do. ..	6,000	3,780
3	Erasers, India rubber, imported	Dozen ..	137 dozen, 4 pieces.	112 dozen, 4 pieces.
4	Gum, Arabic, imported	lb. ..	89½	88
5	Hones, local	Number	9	....
6	Ink—			
	(a) Fluid in 40 oz. jars, blue-black, local ..	Do. ..	6	6
	(b) Do. red, do.	Do. ..	3	3
	(c) Powders (to make 24 oz. fluid ink, blue-black, local).	Do. ..	600	364
	(d) Powders (to make 24 oz. fluid ink, red, local).	Do. ..	21	21
7	Inkstand, wooden, double, local	Do. ..	9	9
8	Knives (desk-knives), local	Do. ..	120	105
9	Needles, large, imported	Do. ..	200	197
10	Nibs for steel pens, imported—			
	(a) Red ink	Gross ..	48	28½
	(b) Relief	Do. ..	24	18½
11	Paper—			
	(a) Bleached double foolscap 27″×17″, 20 lb., local.	Ream ..	33	31 reams, 400 sheets.
	(b) Do. 16 lb., do.	Do. ..	36	35 reams, 150 sheets.
	(c) Blotting, white, demy 22½″ × 17½″, 40 lb., local.	Quire ..	100	58 quires, 18 sheets.
	(d) Brown cartridge, super royal 29″ × 22″, 30 lb., local.	Ream ..	30 reams, 250 sheets.	24 reams, 350 sheets.
	(e) Unbleached, double foolscap 27″ × 17″, 16 lb., local.	Do. ..	10 reams, 250 sheets.	10 reams, 250 sheets.
12	Pencils—			
	(a) Blue, imported	Number ..	121	119
	(b) Lead Do.	Gross ..	275	177
	(c) Red Do.	Number ..	61	56
13	Penholders, clerical, local	Dozen ..	72	65 dozen, 1 holder.
14	Pins, imported	Do. ..	24 dozen, 6 packets.	21 dozen, 1 packet.
15	Rulers, round, 18″, local	Number ..	24	24
16	Scissors, local	Do. ..	12	12
17	Sealing wax, local	Box ..	12	8 boxes, 4 sticks
18	Strawboards, double foolscap 8d., 31½″ × 18¾″, local.	Number ..	960	927
19	Tags, cotton, local	Do. ..	12,500	12,100
20	Tape, white, ½″ wide, 28 yards a roll, local ..	Roll ..	96	68
21	Thread, cotton, in 2 tola balls, local ..	Ball ..	1,703	1,601
22	Twine, country, local	Lb.	682	671

STATEMENT I.

COPYING THE SLIPS.

Office.	Population dealt with.	Number of copyists.	Date of Commencement.	Date of Completion.	Average daily outturn per head.
(1)	(2)	(3)	(4)	(5)	(6)
1. Berhampur	6,019,567	200	16th March 1931.	20th June 1931.	703
2. Rajahmundry	6,433,506	230	23rd March 1931.	30th May 1931 ..	914
3. Bellary	6,662,828	200	18th March 1931.	1st May 1931 ..	816
4. Madras	2,471,978	250	12th March 1931.	13th April 1931 ..	509
5. Tiruvannamalai ..	7,081,341	230	18th March 1931.	31st May 1931 ..	1,051
6. Cannanore	3,533,944	120	16th March 1931.	16th May 1931 ..	613
7. Mangalore	1,925,710	80	16th March 1931.	30th May 1931 ..	610
8. Tanjore I	6,753,672	200	16th March 1931.	6th June 1931 ..	867
9. Tanjore II	6,073,689	200	18th March 1931.	18th May 1931 ..	775

STATEMENT II.

SORTING.

Period up to the end of	Number of units sorted for Table No. VII	VI	XII	VIII	X	XIV	IX
May 1931 ..	59	23	3	23	19	6	3
June " ..	173	132	8	98	86	10	8
July " ..	182	174	12	96	84	9	8
August " ..	28	101	5	142	98	3	9
September " ..	..	12	..	77	110	..	..
October " ..	..	..	..	6	45	..	..
Total ..	442	442	28	442	442	28	28

Remarks.

1. For Tables IX, and XIV the *district* is the unit of sorting; for all others the *taluk* or *town*.
2. Tables (old notation) XIII, XV and XIV originally prescribed were either omitted or were not compiled for Madras.

CHAPTER III.

FINANCE.

THE principles governing the financial side of the 1931 census differed radically from those of earlier years. So extreme are the differences that comparisons with the figures for these years cannot but mislead unless great care is taken.

2. The fundamental difference was that all census expenditure was taken to be a central debit. This was given rigorous application by the local Government and by the Accountant-General. In this they were but logical. The budget, however, drawn up for me by the Madras Government for 1930–31 took no account of this change and in fact merely followed the 1921 figures. Incidentally it was left to the Finance department to point out that 1921 actuals would be a better starting point than the 1921 original estimate. It is important that the census officer should see the budget prepared for his first year (he himself prepares the others) and have a fuller opportunity of comment. He is generally designated well in advance and this suggestion should ordinarily prove practicable. **Changes in account rules.**

Another outstanding difference was that all receipts and recoveries were treated as 'receipts' and credited to a separate revenue head while at the previous census they were treated as abatement of charges and were thus made available for expenditure. This explains the prescription this time of a separate statement of receipts and recoveries in the report.

3. Instances of the wide divergences between 1921 and 1931, divergences which appeared in the budget abovementioned, were that instead of merely census special pay or allowances being debited to the central head the entire emoluments of every census officer were so debited. Thus instead of my Rs. 300 special pay being the single central debit on my account the whole of my pay was so debited. The same applied to Deputy Superintendents, Personal Assistant and all others. The new debit involved was about Rs. 6,000 per month when all the abstraction offices were in full swing.

Other items newly debited in 1931 were—

(*a*) *Paper for house lists, etc.*—Paper for house lists and rough enumeration schedules had to be obtained from the local stores on payment this time. This cost Rs. 5,500.

(*b*) *Printing.*—No printing was done free for me either by the Government of India Press or by the local Government Press. The total cost of printing was Rs. 4,000 in the former and Rs. 34,000 in the latter, excluding the charges on the printing of Reports and Tables. The accounts in the 1921 Administration Report show no debits for Government Press printing but actually the printing of the report and tables was charged, not however the printing of enumeration schedules.

(*c*) *Forms.*—Even the ordinary accounts and other standard forms for use in my office had to be bought at this census from the Deputy Controller of Forms, Calcutta.

(*d*) *Percentage commission on supplies from the local stationery office.*—The Madras Government Stationery office charged me ten per cent commission on the value of all their supplies for census purposes. The amount involved was over Rs. 500.

(*e*) *Contribution to passage accounts.*—The census department had to pay monthly contributions to the passage accounts of officers of All-India services deputed for census duty; the cost totalled Rs. 1,500 nearly.

(*f*) *Postage.*—Under the Auditor-General's rules, postage and telegram charges incurred in districts on census business were debitable to the census grant. Only 14 districts took advantage of these rules to present stamp bills for payment from census funds. A good many of these put up reasonable claims; but Ramnad, Tanjore, Malabar and Trichinopoly were exorbitant in their demands. I exercised all possible care and passed the bills only after satisfying myself that claims represented the actual postage used on such of the census correspondence as could not be combined with the ordinary departmental tapals. The total charges were Rs. 1,042 against Rs. 106 in 1921.

Enumeration travelling allowance.

4. The most marked effect was in travelling allowance of enumeration staff. 1921 showed a figure of Rs. 13,882 for this. No details remained illustrating it. This was only to be expected, for in all previous censuses all census travelling by the officers of the local Government, who form the vast majority of the enumeration staff, was treated as debitable like any other travelling, to the local Government. Census travelling by the officers of Central Departments was likewise debited to these departments. In 1931, on the other hand, in obedience to the rules issued by the Auditor-General and expounded by the local Accountant-General every census journey was charged in a separate bill and sent to me for countersignature. Over 26,000 bills came, some of them many pages thick. The gross claims they represented totalled Rs. 3 lakhs nearly. It was early apparent that no strict principles had governed either the claims or in many cases the check applied to them in the districts. The incidence of national financial difficulties and the need for heavy retrenchment decided me to apply at every stage a strict principle of actual expenses. The application of this began with myself, and so far as my own census touring is concerned the net result was considerable debit. Every attempt was made however to ensure that no man should actually be out of pocket over his journeys and where special considerations were shown I did not hesitate to relax the audit. The strain imposed upon my office was very great. Complaints though frequent were on the whole less than I had anticipated and perhaps census officers responded unconsciously to the general principles expounded in communications I made to the local Government and Collectors explaining the reasons for my action—copies of these are in the appendix. Never again however should a census superintendent be put in the position I was of dealing with bills covering all census travelling, and before next census the allocation of debits should go on a natural and practical rather than a purely theoretical basis. The idea that a great national activity like the census can be completely dissociated from the life and responsibilities of the local Government is preposterous. It is precisely to local Governments which are the effective administrative units touching the life of the country, that census figures are most useful and the village statistics which form so important an item in the equipment of any district officer derive directly from the census operations. No doubt the local Government in 1931 paid for the actual cost of extracting these statistics. That extraction however could never have been possible had not the prolonged and costly general census operations been carried through. I suggest that at all future censuses, enumeration charges should be a provincial debit or, at any rate, all payments to enumeration staff should be so debited.

I toured the entire presidency twice during the enumeration stages. Though I invariably limited my claims for travelling allowance during these tours to the actual expenses, payment on my bills was on several occasions delayed for want of technical sanction by the Census Commissioner, which naturally took long to reach me. It is a mordant commentary on audit and its application that it was only because I wanted to save Government money that I had to wait for payment. I could have drawn the full claims in a day. To avoid these difficulties I would suggest that a special scheme be devised at the next census for the payment of travelling allowance to provincial census superintendents. In fact Mr. W. R. Tennant formulated such a scheme for this census but unfortunately it was not sanctioned by the Government of India until after the census enumeration was over. Their sanction was communicated to me as late as 22nd April 1931. Under this scheme the provincial superintendent was to be paid for the four months beginning 1st November 1930, in which the intensity of census inspection was greatest, the following allowances :—

(1) Motor-car allowance of Rs. 100 per month.

(2) Road mileage two annas per mile for journeys outside headquarters, and

(3) Daily allowance if admissible, notwithstanding the drawal of road mileage on the same day, subject to the general condition that the minimum of touring by rail is done.

This scheme is economical and simple and I would commend its timely introduction at least in the next census.

5. Rigid economy was observed throughout. I was not so fortunate in obtaining rentfree accommodation as previous superintendents and one illustration of the change in account procedure was that I had to pay rent for the Sangita Mahal in Tanjore whereas the 1921 census had the same building rentfree. However, by abstaining from long leases I was able to take advantage of the Army Clothing Department building falling vacant in the middle of 1931 and thereby save Rs. 4,000 in rent. Fees were collected from stallkeepers who set up business in the compounds of the abstraction offices and these went to meet incidental expenses. **Economy in expenditure.**

Through the kindness of the Chief Conservator of Forests, Madras, I was spared the necessity of incurring any appreciable charges on my own office furniture and his liberal supply of articles placed me above all wants. My thanks are specially due to him for this.

Printing at private presses was less often resorted to on this occasion. Stray vernacular circulars from certain districts and circle lists that could not be printed in time at the Madras Government Press were all that were entrusted to them. Bills for work costing over Rs. 20 done at these presses were sent to the Deputy Controller of Printing, Calcutta, for scrutiny and sanction. The cost under this head was Rs. 13,907 as against Rs. 17,102 in 1921.

The 1921 accounts show no recoveries from Sandur and Banganapalle States either for the enumeration forms supplied to them or for the abstraction and tabulation of their census figures though presumably such recovery took place. Recoveries were effected in 1931 amounting to Rs. 450 nearly.

6. The apparent increase in cost over 1921 is 6·30 lakhs minus 5·15, or 1·15. This does not however represent the true facts. At the last census no charge was made for Government printing of enumeration schedules. Enumeration travelling allowance claimed by Government servants was not a census debit. Certain other charges debited in 1931 were not debited in 1921, although incurred. The strict comparison would be to add to the 1921 cost debits under the heads now debited for the first time in 1931. The amounts, however, are lost in the provincial finances and cannot now be extracted. Consequently I have taken the alternative course of deducting from the 1931 charges those which were not debited, though incurred, in 1921. Care has been taken to avoid any unduly favourable interpretation. Thus travelling allowance paid to private individuals was paid also in 1921 and has not been taken into account. The contributions to passage account, although not charged in 1921, are not strictly a fresh debit; it was simply because they did not exist in 1921 that that census escaped them. They have not therefore been taken into account. **Cost.**

The figures are—

	RS.	RS.
Gross cost 1931	..	6,30,000
Deduct items not debited in 1921;		
Enumeration travelling allowance to Government servants ..	1,25,000	
Paper for house lists, etc.	5,000	
Ten per cent commission on supplies from local Government's Stationery office	500	
Accounts and standard forms..	200	
Printing of enumeration schedules, etc., at Government Press ..	19,000	
	1,49,700	
Deduct receipts and recoveries treated as abatement of charges to accord with the 1921 procedure	41,500	
Total deductions ..	..	1,91,200
Net cost 1931		4,38,800

The net cost per thousand becomes therefore Rs. 9–5. This is a reduction of almost one-fourth on the 1921 cost of Rs. 12–1. The gross figure is Rs. 13–6 per thousand, about a fifteenth of the cost of the English census. Madras censuses will compare favourably in expense with those of any other country in the world.

APPENDIX.

Copy of letter to the Secretary to Government, Law (General) Department, No. 2410-1, *dated 9th July* 1931.

I enclose a copy of a circular letter I am sending to Collectors, with the following further remarks.

2. I have already brought to your notice the extra work imposed on my office by the change in allocation of census expenditure as between 1921 and 1931. You have already gathered from my letter applying for permission to engage a special travelling allowance clerk, the dimensions of the problem. The bills after passing are being returned by railway parcel to the Collectors of the various districts. This saves a great deal of time, trouble and expense and incidentally will give a further light on the nature of the burden thrown upon my office.

3. Before the urgent calls for retrenchment were sent out I had already exercised a fairly close audit of travelling allowance because my budget grants were far from ample. I applied to all census travelling allowance the principle of reasonable actual expenditure instead of a mere following of technical allowance rules. I have myself from the first claimed travelling allowance strictly on an actual expense basis, and I am in fact out of pocket over my census journeys. This however has enabled me to apply freely in the case of others considerations that have throughout governed my own case. I enclose a copy of a typical endorsement given to officers whose subordinates had protested against the application of my audit. It was quite clear from an early stage that exaggerated claims were going to be frequent and that no strict district audit was to be expected. Many a time have I come across the remarkable phenomenon that the rate of bandy hire in the same town varied considerably but was always equal to the rate of mileage which the particular traveller could under the rules claim in the case of long journeys. One man in Poonamallee claimed mileage for a journey of two miles from his headquarters. Men in Malabar have shown 28 days' census touring in a month, the day's distance travelled being by an odd coincidence just over five miles from headquarters. I do not mention these as complaints but merely to show the sort of problem I was up against in my desire to secure economy and bring expenditure within my funds. Roughly I have tried to deal with every bill on its own merits and to ensure that while expenditure was cut down to a minimum, every person who made a census journey was recouped for his efforts and expenses incurred.

4. The Government of India instruction, dated 18th December 1930, that wherever possible census work should be combined with ordinary touring does not seem to have received the attention which was its due. Consequently I refused to pass any census travelling allowance bill of a touring officer for journeys within his jurisdiction, unless special reasons were shown.

5. With the consent of the Census Commissioner I have issued orders declining to consider any bills for travelling allowance during the enumeration stage, received after the 30th June 1931. Since the order was issued, 200 bills have come and a few arrive every day. I propose to disregard these. There can have been no census journey since the end of February and four months is surely ample time to await receipt of claims.

6. The only other province in which this problem has occurred is Assam. Bengal and United Provinces know it not. How they escaped this welter of bills I do not know; possibly, their local Governments were not so quick to seize the implications of the audit separation. I have told the Census Commissioner that I do not think that a provincial Superintendent should be put in the position in which I have been, of auditing thousands of bills from all over the presidency. It seems, I am afraid, certain that a reasonable district audit cannot be expected and had I not taken these bills to my own audit, the total claims would have been in the neighbourhood of not 1 lakh but 3 or 4.

7. I fully anticipate a considerable crop of objections and complaints against a rather drastic audit and where any definite hardship is made out I have always tried to meet it. In all other cases I have maintained my audit system.

ENCLOSURE I.

OFFICE OF THE SUPERINTENDENT OF CENSUS OPERATIONS, MADRAS.
Mount Road, the 3rd July 1931.

Letter No. 2052-4.

From

M. W. W. M. YEATTS, Esq., I.C.S.,
SUPERINTENDENT OF CENSUS OPERATIONS,
Madras,

To

ALL COLLECTORS.

SIR,

[Enumeration—Travelling allowance claims.]

I frequently receive reminders from persons who claimed travelling allowance for journeys performed as census officers during the enumeration stages. I should like to explain the causes which have led to the delay in returning these bills.

(1) The enormous number concerned and the absence of any staff to deal with them. The total bills received number 26,000 and only one clerk is available.

(2) A large cut in the budget produced the effect that by the middle of May the funds were exhausted and until fresh funds were secured, no bills could be passed. A further grant has been obtained and bills are being dealt with and sent out as quickly as possible.

(3) In view of the serious financial condition, and it must be said, a very common lack of restraint in the claims, a stringent audit has had to be applied, which tended to increase the time. This audit has taken as its guiding principle, the theory expressed in frequent endorsements on earlier bills, a theory which has been uniformly followed in my own case.

I have the honour to be,
Sir,
Your most obedient servant,

T. B. SUBRAHMANYAM,
For *Superintendent of Census Operations.*

ENCLOSURE II.

Copy of Endorsement.

Census is a piece of public service in the interests of the whole community and officials and non-officials alike are expected to give their help free wherever possible. I cannot therefore pass the bill for more than what I consider to be reasonable actual expenses, even though the ordinary travelling allowance rules may allow your claims in full.

I.—Expenditure distributed under the heads prescribed by the Census Commissioner.

Main head.	Sub-head.	1930–31.	1931–32.	*1932–33.	Total 1930–33.
		RS.	RS.	RS.	RS.
A. SUPERINTENDENCE.					
	A. 1. Pay of Officers.				
	1. Pay of officers	16,969	16,956	4,192	38,117
	2. Deputation allowance of officers.	3,200	3,510	864	7,574
	Total A. 1. (Non-voted) ..	20,169	20,466	5,056	45,691
	A. 2. Pay of Establishment.				
	3. Superintendent's office	..	..	..	..
	3. a. (i) Pay of men deputed to census duty	2,207	2,616	885	5,708
	3. a. (ii) Duty allowance of men of deputation for census ..	889	1,098	353	2,340
	3. b. Pay of men without substantive appointments. .	1,685	2,463	737	4,885
	Total A. 2. (Voted) ..	4,781	6,177	1,975	12,933
	A. 3. Allowances, Honoraria, etc.				
	4. Travelling and other allowances	..	..	..	..
	4. a. Officers (Non-voted)	5,990	2,878	..	8,868
	4. b. Establishment (Voted) ..	295	216	..	511
	4. c. Other allowances to establishment	..	..	..	..
	Total A. 3. Voted ..	295	216	..	511
	Total A. 3. Non-voted ..	5,990	2,878	..	8,868
	A. 4. Contingencies.				
	5. a. Office rent	249	..	..	249
	b. Purchase and repair of furniture	228	47	..	275
	c. Stationery	521	21	19	561
	d. Postage and telegram charges.	950	651	50	1,651
	e. Freight	167	233	20	420
	f. Miscellaneous	343	335	75	753
	g. Telephone charges	187	256	76	519
	h. Rewards	..	..	..	..
	i. Hot and cold weather charges.	1	..	..	1
	j. Purchase of books and maps.	47	34	15	96
	k. Liveries and warm clothing ..	..	..	..	..
	l. Purchase and repair of tents.	..	..	..	..
	m. Camel gear	..	..	..	..
	n. Other contingencies	114	..	..	114
	Total A. 4. Voted ..	2,807	1,577	255	4,639
	A. 5. Grants-in-aid, contribution, etc.				
	6. Contributions to passage account	..	1,316	160	1,476
	Total A. 5. Non-voted ..	..	1,316	160	1,476
TOTAL A ..	Voted ..	7,883	7,970	2,230	18,083
	Non-voted ..	26,159	24,660	5,216	56,035
B. ENUMERATION.	*B. 1. Pay of Establishments.*				
	7. District Office	3,458	937	..	4,395
	8. Remuneration of census officers	988	154	..	1,142
	Total B. 1. Voted ..	4,446	1,091	..	5,537
	B. 2. Allowances, Honoraria, etc.				
	9. Travelling allowance	7,041	1,31,638	1,583	1,40,262
	Total B. 2. Voted ..	7,041	1,31,638	1,583	1,40,262

* Incomplete (up to 15th July 1932 only).

I.—Expenditure distributed under the heads prescribed by the Census Commissioner—cont.

Main head.	Sub-head.	1930-31.	1931-32.	*1932-33.	Total 1930-33.
		RS.	RS.	RS.	RS.
	B. 3. Contingencies.				
	10. a. Stationery	337	95	..	432
	b. Postage and telegram charges.	897	145	..	1,042
	c. House-numbering charges ..	1,065	859	..	1,924
	d. Freight	172	58	..	230
	e. Miscellaneous	1,119	337	1	1,457
	Total B. 3. Voted ..	3,590	1,494	1	5,085
TOTAL B ..	Voted ..	15,077	1,34,223	1,584	1,50,884
C. ABSTRACTION AND COMPILATION.					
	C. 1. Pay of officers.				
	11. Pay of officers	..	3,026	..	3,026
	Total C. 1. Voted ..	..	3,026	..	3,026
	C. 2. Pay of establishment.				
	12. Working staff including Superintendence—				
	a. Officials	612	41,903	1,328	46,843
	b. Non-officials	..	1,93,749	2,748	1,96,497
	Total C. 2. Voted ..	612	2,38,652	4,076	2,43,340
	C. 3. Allowances, Honoraria, etc.				
	13. Travelling allowance ..	1,443	2,369	15	3,827
	Total C. 3. Voted ..	1,443	2,369	15	3,827
	C. 4. Contingencies.				
	14. a. Office rent	175	6,345	..	6,520
	b. Purchase and repair of furniture	17,384	1,692	..	19,076
	c. Stationery	..	173	1	174
	d. Postage and telegram charges.	150	568	..	718
	e. Freight	958	1,321	..	2,279
	f. Miscellaneous	430	1,950	132	2,512
	g. Petty construction	646	..	..	646
	h. Hot and cold weather charges.	..	50	..	50
	i. Liveries	..	..	..	..
	j. Rewards	..	..	..	..
	Total C. 4. Voted ..	19,743	12,099	133	31,975
TOTAL C ..	Voted ..	21,798	2,56,146	4,224	2,82,168
D. MISCELLANEOUS STAFF.					
	15. Officers	..	..	..	..
	16. Establishment	6,035	494	..	6,529
	17. Other allowances	..	..	..	..
TOTAL D ..	Voted ..	6,035	494	..	6,529
E. PRINTING AND OTHER STATIONERY CHARGES.					
	18. Enumeration :				
	(i) Printing (*a*) at Government Press ..	17,868	5,656	..	23,524
	(*b*) at private presses.	13,907	..	..	13,907
	(ii) Other charges	25,142	525	..	25,667
	19. Abstraction and compilation—				
	(i) Printing (*a*) at Government Presses ..	2,192	17,035	4,700	23,927
	(*b*) at private presses ..	..	..	..	..
	(ii) Other charges	13,722	1,708	1,197	16,627
TOTAL E ..	Voted ..	72,831	24,924	5,897	1,03,652
	Grand total ..	1,49,783	4,48,417	19,151	6,17,351
Grand total ..	Voted ..	1,23,624	4,23,757	13,935	5,61,316
	Non-voted ..	26,159	24,660	5,216	56,035

* Incomplete (up to 15th July 1932 only).

II.—A. Recoveries and B. Receipts credited to the Central Government under "Census."

Account.	1930-31.	1931-32.	1932-33.	Total 1930-33.	Remarks.
A.—RECOVERIES.					
(i) From Indian States.					
	RS. A. P.	RS. A. P.	RS. A. P.	RS. A. P.	
Cost of forms supplied to Cochin	..	1,318 7 0	..	1,318 7 0	
Do. Pudukkottai	..	486 10 0	..	486 10 0	
Do. Sandur	..	21 9 0	..	21 9 0	
Do. Banganapalle	..	25 14 0	..	25 14 0	
Cost of abstraction and compilation recovered from Sandur	..	100 0 0	..	100 0 0	
Cost of abstraction and compilation recovered from Banganapalle	..	290 0 0	..	290 0 0	
Total (i) ..	..	2,242 8 0	..	2,242 8 0	
(ii) From Municipalities and Local Boards.					
Cost of forms supplied to Madras Corporation ..	..	..	151 2 0	151 2 0	
Cost of abstraction and compilation recovered from Madras Corporation	..	..	2,386 10 0	2,386 10 0	
Cost of abstraction and compilation recovered from district municipalities	..	27,501 6 0	572 3 0	28,073 9 0	
Cost of abstraction and compilation recovered from Coorg municipalities	..	88 7 0	..	88 7 0	
Cost of light, ink, petty stationery, etc., used in district board areas	* 525 0 0	..	..	525 0 0	* District boards were as a rule asked to meet these charges from the very beginning but certain boards did not do so and only in their cases were recoveries made.
Total (ii) ..	525 0 0	27,589 13 0	3,109 15 0	31,224 12 0	
(iii) Miscellaneous.					
Cost of preparation of village statistics recovered from Madras Government	..	2,600 0 0	..	2,600 0 0	
Cost of preparation of village statistics recovered from Coorg Province	..	..	20 0 0	20 0 0	
Cost of preparation of Provincial Table 3 recovered from Madras Government	..	..	200 0 0	200 0 0	
Excess travelling allowance recovered from Government servants	..	98 13 0	..	98 13 0	
Total (iii) ..	..	2,698 13 0	220 0 0	2,918 13 0	
Total A.—Recoveries ..	525 0 0	32,531 2 0	3,329 15 0	36,386 1 0	Rs. 6,000 being the cost of special work done for the Orissa Boundary Committee was recovered from the committee and treated as abatement of charges as an exceptional case.
B.—RECEIPTS.					
Sale-proceeds of schedule paper, slips and other forms	3 6 0	..	10 0 0	13 6 0	
Sale-proceeds of furniture	..	3,905 15 6	297 5 3	4,203 4 9	
Sale-proceeds of typewriting machine and other stationery articles	..	308 1 7	220 2 3	528 6 10	
Total B.—Receipts ..	3 6 0	4,214 4 1	527 7 6	4,745 1 7	
Grand Total ..	528 6 0	36,745 6 1	3,857 6 6	41,131 2 7	